GANESHA
The Auspicious . . . The Beginning

Dedicated to

SEETHA

sister and aunt
who was born on Ganesh Chaturthi Day
and left this earth on the same day
25 years later

S.J. & N.K.

Cover
Ganesha
Tanjore Painting, 18th *c.*

GANESHA

The Auspicious . . . The Beginning

Shakunthala Jagannathan
Nanditha Krishna

Vakils, Feffer & Simons Pvt. Ltd.
Industry Manor, Appasaheb Marathe Marg
Prabhadevi, Mumbai - 400 025, India

Credits

Photography:
V. K. Rajamani

Line Drawings:
P. Ramasamy
Y. Venkatesh

Photographs made available through the courtesy of:
Archaeological Survey of India
Thiruvaduthurai Aadheenam
Usha Bhatia
Vakil & Sons Pvt. Ltd., Mumbai

Icons, paintings, carvings kindly provided by:
M. Deenadayalu, Aparna Art Gallery, Chennai (cover page)
Tushar Mehta, Nirmala Seshadri, Devaki Muthiah,
Jaya Chandrasekhar, Sujata Chittiappa, Shobha Hebbar

First printing 1992   Second printing 1995
Third Printing 1996   Fourth Printing 2000
Fifth Printing 2002   Sixth Printing 2003
Seventh Printing 2006   Eighth Printing 2008

Price in India Rs. 395/-

Published by Bimal Mehta
for Vakils, Feffer and Simons Pvt. Ltd.
Industry Manor, Appasaheb Marathe Marg
Prabhadevi, Mumbai 400 025, India

Printed by Arun K. Mehta at Vakil & Sons Pvt. Ltd.
Industry Manor, Appasaheb Marathe Marg
Prabhadevi, Mumbai 400 025, India

ISBN 978-81-8462-004-7

Web site : www.vakilspublications.com
E-mail   : info@vakilspublications.com
Phone   : 91-22-2430 6780
Fax   : 91-22-2422 5111

Contents

Note on Spellings

Wherever possible phonetic spellings have been used to help readers who are not familiar with the more unusual words e.g. Gajamukhaasura , Phaalachandra, paasha, etc. However familiar words like Vinayaka, Naga, avatar, ect. are spelt as they are popularly spelt and not phonetically.

In the case of Sanskrit shlokas, transcribed in English, ट is written in English as ta, ठ as tta, त as tha, and थ as thha.

In the English text of the book however, it is used for both ट and त as used in the rest of India (and not as in South India where ट is spelt as ta and त as tha).

Preface

To write a book on Ganesha requires the wisdom of Ganesha and his courage, neither of which I can even remotely claim to possess.

However the study of Ganesha has fascinated me and dogged my mind for years, but research on the subject, with limited source material, was not easy. I was greatly assisted in this by my daughter, Nanditha Krishna, an art historian, and we put together this book as a result of our separate and joint researches.

We are greatly indebted to the various spiritual heads, researchers and authors of books whose publications aided us in our research.

So many kind persons helped us in our endeavour and I cannot adequately express my gratitude to them.

V.K. Rajamani spared hours of his valuable time, and his excellent photography has embellished the book, as have P. Ramasamy's and Y. Venkatesh's line drawings.

The Thiruvaduthurai Aadheenam very kindly permitted the use of their photographs and drawings and the Archaeological Survey of India provided photographs as did Usha Bhatia. Arun Mehta furnished prints of paintings from Vakils collection.

Prof. P.R. Vaidyanatha Sastri, Vimala Krishnamurti and Sundari Mani aided me in locating source material in Sanskrit and Tamil.

My cousin, P.C. Ramakrishna, helped to select the title of the book.

Private collections of Ganesha images, paintings, photographs and prints were kindly made available to me to illustrate the book.

I would particularly like to mention Tushar Mehta's collection of bronzes.

M. Deenadayalu of Aparna Art Gallery, Madras, loaned the antique Tanjore Ganesha of the cover page, from his personal collection.

My father, Shri C.R. Pattabhi Raman, my daughter Nanditha, and friends, Nirmala Seshadri, Devaki Muthiah and Shobha Hebbar, amongst others gave me interesting icons and paintings from their collections for the book. Artists Jaya Chandrasekhar and Sujata Chittiappa loaned their own creations, the Tanjore painting, Vishwaroopa Ganapati and the Mysore painting, Seated Ganesha.

I should also like to thank so many others — T.S. Jaya, B. Sheela, Malathi Narasimhan, O.R. Padmanabhan, S. Sumathra, K. Shantha, V. Shanthi, S. Ravi and M. Sekhar — for their invaluable help. But for all of them this book could never have been completed.

Shakunthala Jagannathan

Madras

Foreword

वेदाहमेतं पुरुषम्महान्तं आदित्यवर्णम्

One of the many glories of Hinduism consists in the tremendously wide variety of divine manifestations that it has conceived down the log corridors of time since the dawn of history. The Hindu pantheon is rich with various deities, all of them manifestations of the same divine Brahman, and all powerful pathways to salvation.

Among the many deities worshipped by the Hindus, Lord Ganesha has in some ways pride of place. It is not that he is considered to be superior to the great Gods Lord Shiva and Lord Vishnu, or the Goddesses, but he has a special place in the affection of people and no worship of any kind or of any other deity can begin without an initial worship to Ganesha, among whose many names is Vighneshwara, remover of obstacles.

In this book, Shakunthala Jagannathan and her daughter Nanditha Krishna have produced an excellent volume on the varied symbology, mythology and iconography of Ganesha. In my view, one of the more important aspects is that Ganesha's elephant head in a way describes the symbol for AUM, which is considered the most sacred word in Hindu literature and is looked upon as the audio-visual representation of the divine. His worship at the beginning of any ritual would thus be a reminder that what we are really worshipping is not the image as such, but the all-pervasive divine power that stands behind it.

Shrimati Jagannathan's earlier book on Hinduism was well received in India and abroad, and I am sure that this one will be equally, if not more, popular.

May Lord Ganesha shower his blessings upto us all, and remove the many obstacles that we face individually and collectively as the world moves rapidly towards the end of this millennium.

New Delhi
1 June 1992

Dr. Karan Singh

Sandstone Ganesha, U.P., 10th *c.*

Ganesha, the Ultimate Reality

At the end of the last age, there had been a *pralaya*, a great deluge, which had destroyed the Universe as it existed then. This was followed by the long, long night of Brahma, when there was pitch darkness everywhere, a great stillness, no sound, no movement, only peace, peace, peace.

Suddenly there was a little rustling, a feeling of expectancy that something great was about to happen. The night of Brahma stretching to 4320 million human years was about to come to a close. Creation has no beginning nor end. It is *anaadi*, eternal, and a day of Brahma was to dawn anew following the long night.

Through this still night suddenly emerged a beautiful sound, a powerful sound, the mind-blowing sound of OM*. In this new age, called the Shwetavaraha Kalpa, the Great God had appeared in the form of OM to recreate a new world. The vibrations of OM were followed by a beautiful soft light, the first dawn heralding a new Sun.

The Great God, the Supreme Spirit, called to his presence the Trinity, Brahma, Vishnu and Rudra-Shiva, and gave Brahma the task of creation.

Brahma was confused and at a loss as to what he should do next and meditated on the Great God. Out of the vibrations of the sound of OM, the Lord of all the worlds conceived the four Vedas, the Rig, Yajur, Sama and Atharva, and taught the knowledge from these books to Brahma who then created our present Universe, the world in which we live, and many other worlds beyond.

However the Ganapatya Cult (which was later absorbed into Hinduism), believes that OM or the Pranava Mantra as this symbol of God is called, is embodied in the form of Ganesha, also commonly known as Ganapati or Vinayaka. He is the first Word, *Vaak*, the First Cause.

According to this cult, with the sound of OM resounding through the Universe, Ganesha appeared against the light of the first dawn, blowing the conch through which the sound of OM had emanated. He came in the form of Nritya Ganapati, dancing in great abandon, swirling, whirling, his movements beyond Man's understanding. He called the Trinity to him and asked them to create and preserve the world and to destroy the evils in it.

But they were confused as to what they should do and how to do it. Ganesha told them he was the Universe itself and swallowed them, and asked them to see all the worlds reflected inside him and to meditate on them.

Brahma even then found he was unable to create the world or the beings in it as they should be created. Ganesha

Shuklaambaradharam vishnum
Shashivarnam chaturbhujam
Prasannavadanam dhyaayeth
Sarvavighnopashaantaye

He who is attired in a white garment
Who is all-pervading and has the complexion of the moon
Who has four arms and a bright and gracious countenance
On him we meditate for the removal of obstacles

---

* Pronounced OHM. Also spelt AUM

OM in Tamil

appeared before him and chastised him, saying that he was not able to achieve the role given to him as he had not first meditated on Ganapati, nor on the symbol of God, OM, which Ganesha symbolised.

Brahma then meditated on Ganapati who asked the goddesses, Siddhi (Achievement) and Buddhi (Wisdom) to help Brahma. And with their help, the Universe in all its beauty came into being. The gods and all the worlds rejoiced and sang —

OM! Praise be to thee, Oh Ganapati!

Thou art the Ultimate Reality, the One Truth

Thou art Brahma the Creator, Vishnu the Preserver,

Rudra-Shiva, the Destroyer, the Supreme Brahman, the Manifest Spirit

The Universe is born from Thee

The elements — earth, water, fire, air and ether, are manifest in Thee

We meditate on Thy countenance, enlighten therefore our powers of understanding

Thou art the Eternal Brahman! OM!

Thus, according to the Ganapatyas, was the present Universe created, and with it the present age, the Shwetavaraha Kalpa, dawned.

OM Shri Ganeshaaya Namah — so begins the prayer to Ganapati, the son of Shiva and Parvati, possibly the most interesting deity in the Hindu pantheon and the iconologist's delight.

Through the length and breadth of this sub-continent, especially in the southern and western regions, a prayer to Ganesha precedes all worship and nothing auspicious can take place without invoking his name.

A child is first introduced to learning with a prayer to Ganesha, the fountain-head of wisdom. When laying the foundation of a building, Ganesha is invoked before placing the first stone. No new business or industry is started without a prayer to him. Travellers on lonely roads stop and pray at roadside Ganesha shrines comforting themselves that Ganapati will remove all dangers in their path. At the foot and at the top of hills and mountains there are stone figures of Ganesha to make the path of the wayfarer smooth and free from obstacles. In Tamil Nadu, when two roads meet at a dead-end, a Ganesha image is installed at the junction for prevention of accidents.

All auspicious events begin with an invocation to this deity. Images of Ganesha are therefore found everywhere — on pavements in towns and cities, at the entrance to villages, in small shrines inside large temples dedicated to other deities, next to carvings of the Saptamatrika (the seven minor mother goddesses), as carvings on pillars, and near Naga or snake stones under the *peepul,* banyan and other sacred trees.

At the commencement of all *samskaras* or rituals that dot the life of a Hindu from birth until the evening of his life, it is the worship of Ganesha that precedes the ceremony. For Ganesha is the remover of obstacles in one's path, the guarantor of success in all ventures. It is believed that one who worships him need never fear failure. He gives knowledge to the seeker of wisdom, prosperity to those who search for worldly gains, progeny to the childless and the path of *moksha* (salvation) to those in search of spiritual liberation.

Possibly Ganesha is the most beloved of all deities of the Hindu pantheon. He is accepted by all the various cults, and the schism which often divides Shaivites and Vaishnavites does not affect him. He is accepted as the first divinity to be worshipped by both and sometimes a small shrine of Ganesha is seen in Vishnu temples also.

Even more important is his adaptability in the modern context. There are no strict or rigid rules or canons of the Shastras binding down his worship as has happened in the case of other deities. He can be worshipped in any form, even as a small triangular pyramid of turmeric, if his icon is

Agajaanana padmaarkam Gajaananam aharnisham

Anekadam tham bhakthaanaam ekadantham upaasmahe

To the elephant-faced one on seeing whom his mother Parvati's face lights up

Just as the lotus blooms at the sight of the rising sun

To that Gajaanana do we pray night and day

To the one with the single tusk who grants many boons to his devotees

To that Ekadanta do we pray night and day

3

not available. It is this adaptability which made Lokamanya Tilak choose Ganesh Chaturthi to unify people in nationalistic endeavour during the freedom struggle. It is again this adaptability which we see in tableaux put up during the Ganapati festival in Maharashtra when this deity is surrounded by astronauts who visited the moon or has space rockets around him. He is made part and parcel of contemporary events and new legends are built around him in these tableaux.

Ganesha, again unlike other gods, is conceived as the worshipper desires and is not strait-jacketed by narrow rituals or bound down by tradition.

The qualities assigned to him moreover are very child-like, and therefore loveable. Possibly the young Ganesha and the child Krishna are the only two deities whom every woman would like to feel are her own sons, playful and mischievous yet harmless and highly attractive. The child

Dancing Ganesha, Gurjara Pratihara·
Kanauj, 9th *c.*

4

Ganesha's fat and podgy arms make him a very bonny child, just asking to be cuddled. His nature as a benefactor of his devotees has made him beloved of all.

Most astonishing is the form of this god. Imagine how a real elephant's head would look on a short, fat human body! Yet how exquisitely they have been proportioned, and put together with such grace and artistry that the sheer beauty of Ganesha is breathtaking. His elephant head, his dwarfish body with a huge paunch, his short and fat arms and legs do not elicit any feeling other than sheer wonder and adoration.

Ganesha is addressed in hymns and prayers by many names, sometimes eight, sometimes twelve, sometimes sixteen, sometimes thirty-two. Most popularly he is addressed as Ganapati or Ganesha, lord of the *ganas* or celestial hordes, and as Gajaanana, the one with the face of an elephant. He is also called Vakratunda of the twisted trunk, and Ekadanta, having but one tusk. He is known as Krishna Pingaaksha, one with dark, reddish brown eyes and Gajavaktra, having an elephant's mouth. He is Lambodara, one with a fat belly, and Vikata, of the monstrous figure. He is addressed as Vighnaraja and Vighneshwara, the king and lord of obstacles as also Vignaharta or Vighnanaashin, the destroyer of obstacles. His smoke-coloured body has given him the name, Dhoomravarna, and his tawny colour, the name Kapila. He is Phaalachandra, sporting the moon crest, and Vinayaka, remover of hindrances.

He is also Sumukha, of the auspicious and pleasant visage, Heramba, the five-headed protector of the weak, and Ganaadhyaksha, the leader of the celestial hordes. His large ears resemble the winnow and have given him the name, Soorpakarna. He is Skandapoorvaja, older than Skanda, the other son of Shiva and Parvati. He is Akhuratha, with the rat as his chariot, and Siddhidaata, the bestower of success. The Tamils however have their own special name for him — Pillaiyar, the revered and noble son.

Whatever the name by which he is addressed, all prayers to Ganesha ask for the removal of obstacles which block the path of the devotee, and for success in all endeavours, whatever be the goal.

A common prayer to Ganapati beseeches him thus:

Vakrathunda mahaakaaya
Sooryakoti samaprabhaa
Nirvighnam kurumedeva
Sarvakaaryeshu sarvadaa

(You of the twisted trunk and the massive body
With the dazzle and light of millions of suns
Lead me on a path that has no obstacles nor hindrances
Clearing the way in all that I do, ever, and always!)

Ganesha
Tanjore Glass Painting, 19th *c*.

Ganesha, as the remover of obstacles and the deity first worshippped before any other, has, naturally, a wealth of legends and parables which explain his importance, the extent of his powers and the reasons for his popularity. For these we have to turn to Puranic lore and examine Ganesha's place in the Hindu pantheon.

God in Hinduism

The fundamental tenet of the Hindu faith is the belief in the One God, who is known as the Brahman, the Absolute, the Universal Soul, or the Manifest Spirit. The Brahman is immanent, within and about us, transcendent, outside material existence, transcending Time and Space, and Nirguna, without shape or form. Since this Universal Spirit is formless, it is not considered male or female and is referred to by the impersonal pronoun, Tat (meaning That). All meditation and prayer begin and end with the words, Om Tat Sat, reminding us of the Great God, That Eternal Truth, That Eternal Reality. This Great Power is also called Sat-Chit-Ananda, to remind us that the Brahman, the Ultimate Reality is the Highest Intelligence and is Supreme Bliss.

The mystic syllable, OM, is the symbol of the Brahman, the Great God, and is also known as the Pranava. This sacred word encompasses the whole Universe and goes beyond the periphery of Time itself. It is therefore used at the beginning and end of meditation or prayer, and at all times when the thought of the Brahman pervades the mind and heart.

However, to ordinary mortals, Nirguna Brahman without form is beyond comprehension. Therefore, we have the Saguna Brahman, the Great God, with form and attributes, known as Ishwara, for the guidance of those less spiritually developed and for the average man and woman.

In the early stages of Hindu civilization, the Saguna Brahman, Ishwara, was represented by the Trinity, Brahma, Vishnu and Rudra-Shiva, when they took over the three main functions of God-head, Creation, Preservation and Destruction of the Universe, with the aid of their consorts, Saraswati, Lakshmi and Parvati (Shakti).

However, with its fundamental belief, *Ekam Sat, viprah bahudha vadanti* (the Great God is One, the learned call Him by different names), Hinduism adopted and assimilated the religious beliefs of all the tribes and peoples with whom the early Vedic people came into contact. Each of these groups had its own gods and beliefs, rituals and rites. Some had totemistic deities (gods with animal and bird masks on their heads), and others had deities with several arms and hands, each symbolic of a specific power of the deity being worshipped.

Different scriptures were followed by people according to the different levels of comprehension. The Srutis (the Vedas and the Upanishads), were purely for intellectually evolved persons and aimed at attainment of the Brahman through spiritual enlightenment and Gnyana Yoga or the path of knowledge and wisdom.

The masses however depended on stories from the great epics, the Ramayana and the Mahabharata, as also from the plethora of legends and stories recounted in the Puranas.

The Puranas

The Puranas, eighteen in number, and the Upa Puranas (or subsidiary Puranas) form part of the cornucopia of spiritual literature available to the followers of the Hindu faith. These books are not meant for the scholar, the intellectual or the spiritually evolved, but consist of legends of gods and men which convey the essence of the Vedas, the primary authorities of Hinduism, and the Dharma Shastras (laws governing righteous conduct). Told to children, to the simple villager, to the illiterate and uneducated, these Puranic stories have formed the very basis of the religious education of the masses, conveying by means of short stories the fundamental truths of religion and morality and of what is good and evil. These books also provide ideals to inspire people to raise themselves and perform acts of greatness or aspire to exemplary behaviour, each deity presenting an ideal to be copied and followed.

The Puranas, much later in age than the Vedas and Upanishads, are revelations of Rishis (sages) who conveyed their messages to the masses in an understandable and acceptable form. All the Puranas are attributed to Rishi Vyasa, but as they have been compiled at different periods, it is plausible that they were compiled by different sages but attributed to Vyasa, the most respected of them all.

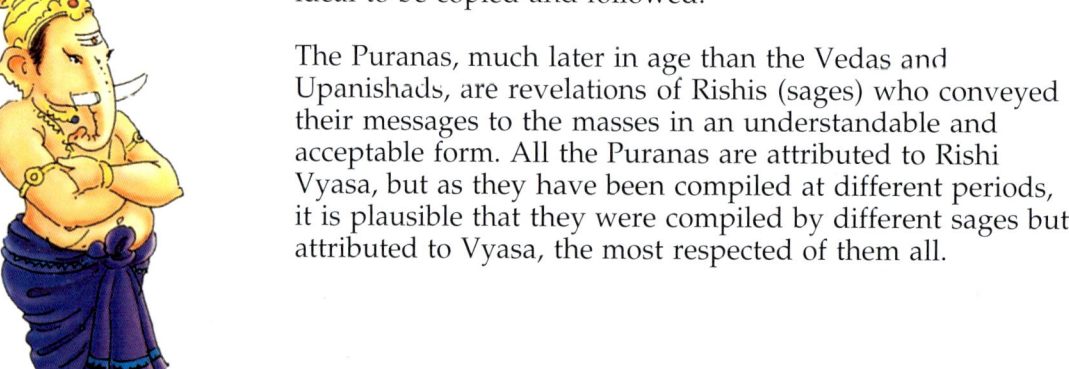

The truths, as revealed by the sages, were conveyed as parables, allegories and legends. Myriads of gods and goddesses of the various local tribes and peoples not mentioned in the Vedas, Smritis or the Epics, found place in the Puranas, however emphasising that, ultimately, all gods and divinities are but different aspects of the one Brahman, the Great God, or his manifestation as one of the Trinity. Puranic stories dealing with different incarnations of divinity or with the Trinity and their consorts, had necessarily to be couched in mystic language and content, but covered all aspects of mundane and worldly behaviour. Qualities of good and evil were encouched in the personalities of gods, demons or human beings. The conflict between good and evil and the humanising of divine beings (even the gods like men make mistakes and get punished), all these aspects make the Puranas easily understood by the masses, and make it possible for them to identify themselves with their gods and goddesses, and the men of evil around them with demons and evil spirits.

Puranic stories are of different types. Some are amusing and comic, representing the culture of a happy people who feel free to laugh and poke fun at their gods.

There are other legends which are sweet and sentimental, and still others which are stern reminders that evil has to be destroyed if good is to prevail.

However, all of them teach the truths and beliefs of the religion in the simplest ways possible, leaving a lasting image in the minds of adults and children.

Ganesha in the Puranas

Since Ganesha has today become one of the most important deities of the Hindu pantheon and has endeared himself to the masses and the elite, it is necessary to acquaint ourselves with the Puranic legends which surround this deity who has been accepted as the son of Shiva and Parvati.

As explained in another chapter, Ganesha in other forms was known as early as 1200 B.C. and was apparently worshipped by several sects in different parts of the country. However images of this deity are only rarely and infrequently seen in art and sculpture till the 4th century A.D.

With the rise in importance of the Ganapatya cult for whom Ganapati was the Supreme God, this deity was absorbed into Hinduism as the son of Shiva and Parvati.

The assimilation was very slow as Ganapati was a folk deity of various pre-Vedic and Tantric sects. (Tantricism was a completely different religion in itself and was not a Hindu sect as often believed).

However the Ganapatya sect was very powerful and widespread and the great philosopher, Adi Shankara himself

Mooshika vaahana modaka hastha
Chaamara karna vilambitha soothra
Vaamana roopa Maheshwara puthra
Vighna Vinaayaka paada namasthe

To him who rides a mouse holding the modaka sweet in his hand

Whose large ears are like fly-whisks and who wears a long sacred thread

Who is short of stature and is the son of Maheshwara

Oh, Vinayaka, lord of obstacles, I bow at your feet!

9

gave them importance by including this sect as one of the six systems (Shanmata) of Hindu worship.

The absorption of Ganesha was achieved through legends and stories in the various Puranas which abound in stories of Ganesha. Although most of the Puranas and Upa Puranas have incidents from the life of Ganesha, the main legends are in the Shiva Purana, Linga Purana, Brahmavaivarta Purana, Skanda Purana, Varaaha Purana, Matsya Purana and Padma Purana and in the two Upa Puranas, the Ganesha Purana and the Mudgala Purana.

These legends refer not only to the birth of Ganesha and his achievements and conquests but also to the miracles by which he acquired his elephant head.

Readers of the Puranas are often confused by different stories regarding the origin of Ganesha, as they appear contradictory. The Shiva Purana explains this by stating that Ganesha originated in different ways in the different *yugas* (ages or time-periods), each time for a different purpose.

However scholars and devotees through the ages have felt that the Puranas have actually belittled the importance of Ganesha by the various legends attached to his birth. To philosophers, Ganesha represents OM, the symbol of the Brahman, also known as the Pranava, the sound from which the world emanated. Ganesha is also the embodiment of *Vaak*, the Word and Kumara, the other son of Shiva and Parvati symbolises Action.

Birth of Ganesha

Each of the Puranas has a different story regarding the birth of Ganesha. In some he is the *maanasika putra* (mind-born son) of Shiva. In others he is the creation of Parvati. In still others he is the son of Shiva and Parvati.

According to one Puranic story, the Devas (minor gods or celestial beings), approached the almighty Shiva and asked for help, as they were being harassed by the demons. Shiva consented to aid them and out of his mind appeared a glorious, glowing figure of a child with the head of a powerful elephant and a trident in one hand. The gods were overjoyed to see the mind-born son of Shiva who would henceforth protect them.

Seeing this beautiful child, Parvati placed him on her lap and vowed that no endeavour, human or divine, would be successful Without a prayer to the young one. Shiva then made him the leader of the *ganas* or celestial hordes, calling him Ganapati.

In another Purana the same story is modified. According to it, Shiva's *maanasika putra* was a dazzling human boy. Parvati, annoyed that the child was born without her intervention, willed that the head should be turned to that of an elephant.

However when she saw the elephant-headed child she felt great love for him, and stated that no endeavour, human or divine, would succeed without a prayer to Ganapati, whom Shiva had made the head of the *ganas*.

A more popular legend deals with the birth of Ganesha to Parvati. Once while Parvati was going for her bath, she rubbed off the dust and oil from her body and out of it created the figure of a young boy. She infused life into the figure and told him he was her son and should guard the entrance when she went down to bathe.

Soon after, Shiva came to see Parvati but the young boy blocked his way and would not let him in. Shiva, unaware that this lad was his son, became furious and in great anger fought with the boy whose head got severed from his body in the ensuing battle. Parvati, returning from her bath, saw her headless son and threatened, as Shakti, to destroy the heavens and the earth, so great was her sorrow.

The gods and Shiva pacified her and the latter sent out his *ganas*, or hordes, to bring the head of the first living being with his head towards the north (the auspicious direction associated with wisdom). They did so and the first living creature they found sleeping with its head to the north was an elephant. They brought the head of this animal and Shiva placed it on the trunk of Parvati's son and breathed life into him.

Parvati was overjoyed and embraced her son, the elephant-headed boy whom Shiva named Ganesha, the lord of his *ganas*.

Another Puranic legend has it that Parvati longed for a child and conveyed her desire to Shiva. He asked her to undertake the Punyaka penance for one year which she did. The sage, Sanatkumara, presided over the austerities and made Parvati undergo several trials and tribulations to test the strength of her vow.

Finally, after she had passed all the tests and completed the vow undertaken by her, she heard a voice from the heavens telling her to look for her new-born son in her chamber. When she ran in and saw the beautiful child, she could not believe her eyes. He was more beautiful than all the gods put together, and his face shone like the morning sun. Her joy knew no bounds.

All the gods and goddesses rushed to Mount Kailas, the abode of the divine parents, to see this child of glory, paid obeisance, and marvelled at the beauty of the child.

The nine *grahas* or planets also came to greet the divine couple and their beloved son. One of them, Shani (Saturn), would not however look up at the child and had his head bent. When Parvati asked him why he was reluctant to look at her son, he told her that there was a curse laid on him by his jealous wife, by which anyone he looked at with admiration would be destroyed.

Parvati, anxious like a fond mother for her son to be admired, insisted that he look at her son.

Shani then looked up at the child whose head immediately got separated from the body and flew off into space. Parvati wailed and lamented so loudly and created such commotion that the gods rushed to Kailas. Vishnu, seeing what had happened to create such grief in Parvati, got on to his vehicle, Garuda, and flew in search of a head to replace the lost one.

On the banks of the River Pushpabhadra, he found a herd of elephants sleeping. Choosing an animal lying with its head to the north, he brought the head of that elephant (who was actually a Gandharva, a celestial being, waiting to be released from earthly life), and placed it on the headless child's neck. Breathing life into the child, he presented it to Parvati who was overjoyed at having a son with the wisdom and power of an elephant.

Vishnu adorned the child with exquisite ornaments to match his beauty, as did Himavaan, the father of Parvati. Vishnu collected all heavenly beings together and led the worship of the child, giving him the eight names by which he came to be commonly known — Vighneshwara, Ganesha, Heramba, Gajaanana, Lambodara, Ekadanta, Soorpakarna and Vinayaka.

Another Puranic legend has it that one day Parvati rubbed oil and sweet smelling powder on her body. Out of the perspiration that came off her body, she created a child. She then lowered the child into the River Ganga. As soon as the

Gajaananam bhoothaganaadi sevitham

Kapithha jamboo phalasaara bhakshitham

Umaasutham shoka vinaasha kaaranam

Namaami Vighneshwara paada pankajam

To the elephant-faced one, served by the hordes of ganas

Who loves the wood-apple and the juice of the rose-apple

Who is the son of Uma and the destroyer of sorrow

Do I bow to the lotus feet of this Vighneshwara, the lord of obstacles

14

waters washed over the child, he grew into a large effulgent being who was now deemed Dvaimatura, the son of two mothers, as Parvati and Ganga each felt he was her son.

Ganapati the child was now given the leadership of the *ganas,* the celestial hordes, by Brahma himself and worshipped in all the three worlds.

All these are stories from the various Puranas where, firstly, Ganesha appears as the son of Shiva or Parvati or both and is given powers as the lord of the *ganas* by Shiva, and secondly, acquires an elephant head which replaces his original human head.

The two Upa Puranas, the Ganesha Purana and the Mudgala Purana on the other hand treat Ganapati as the Great God himself, to whom even the Trinity pay obeisance and ask for his help to save the world from evil.

There are 4 *yugas* or ages, the Krita, Treta, Dwaapara and Kali Yuga. According to the Ganesha Purana, Ganesha incarnated in each *yuga* or age in a different form for a particular purpose.

In the Krita Yuga, Ganesha was born on earth as Mahotkata, the son of sage Kashyapa and his wife Aditi. In this incarnation he destroyed the demons Naraantak and Devaantak who were harassing the three worlds, as also another demon, Dhoomraaksha. On his achieving the purpose of his incarnation, he left his earthly parents, promising them that his astral spirit would be there whenever they wanted him.

In the Treta Yuga, Ganesha was born as a son of Parvati. Once, when playing, he brought a wild peacock under control and was named Mayuresha as a result. He released birds like Jataayu, Shyena and Sampaati from the serpent kingdom and killed the demon Sindhu, the purpose for which he had incarnated. He then married Siddhi and Buddhi (personifications of achievement and wisdom) and gifted his peacock to his brother, Kartikeya, whose vehicle it became. He then went back to his heavenly abode.

In the Dwaapara Yuga, Ganesha was born on earth as Gajaanana, and was adopted by Sage Paraashara and his wife, Vatsala when the king and queen, his parents, deserted him on seeing an elephant-headed child. He then conquered the evil demon, Sindhur, and then taught the Ganesha Geeta, the wisdom of the ages, to the king and queen who had earlier deserted him.

It has been predicted and proved by our own experience that in the Kali Yuga (in which we are living now), evil will predominate. Man will harm his fellow-man, and all beings will chase chimerical values. Desire for wealth and acquisitiveness will lead to all earthly beings destroying one another and bringing about chaos.

To set matters right, the Ganesha Purana avers that Ganesha will incarnate on earth as Dhoomraketu, when he will destroy the evil in the minds of men and reestablish righteousness and peace.

The other Upa Purana, the Mudgala Purana, details eight incarnations of Ganesha, each of which set out to conquer the vices that afflict man and woman and turn their minds away from righteousness.

These vices were given the form of demons whom Ganesha conquers. They also act as lessons to humanity to show that when these vices enter the hearts of men, they are daemonic, overpowering our minds. Such evil has to be destroyed and only then will virtues such as goodness, equanimity and peace take their place in the hearts of mankind.

To conquer the demon of lust, Kaamaasura, Ganesha was born as Vikata and riding the peacock as vehicle, he achieved his life's objective.

He incarnated as Lambodara to vanquish Krodhaasura, the demon of vicious and unjust anger. In this role he rode on his usual vehicle, the mouse.

He subdued the demon of avarice and greed, Lobhaasura, in his birth as Gajaanana.

Mohaasura, the demon of infatuation and delusion was defeated when he assumed the form of Mahodara.

The demon of vanity, Madaasura, was vanquished by Ganesha as Ekadanta.

As Vakratunda, riding a lion, he subdued Maatsara, the demon personifying envy and jealousy.

For removing the demon of attachment and desire, Mamaasura, he assumed the form of Vighnaraja riding Sesha, the celestial serpent.

For the conquest of Abhimaanaasura, the demon of egotistic pride, the role of Dhoomravarna was taken by Ganesha.

In previous ages, assuming various roles, Ganesha conquered and subdued the various vices garbed in daemonic roles. However the fact that these evils have again arisen and are seen around us in all power only shows that we need fresh incarnations of Ganesha to subdue them in this age, the dark age known as Kali Yuga.

Anyathha sharanam naasthi, thvameva sharanam mama

Thasmaath kaarunya bhaavena raksha raksha Vinayaka

I have no other refuge but you
You alone are my saviour
Therefore with compassion
Protect me, oh save me Vinayaka!

17

Other popular legends

In addition to stories of his birth and incarnations, legends about Ganesha are legion. Each part of this vast country has local legends also which enrich the fabric of the lives of those who hear them or read about them.

A few of the better known legends are given below.

Shiva worships Ganapati

It is believed that no act whether of peace or war or daily living will succeed unless Ganesha is worshipped first.

This holds true not only for humans but also for heavenly beings. When Ganesha first appeared as Shiva's mind-born son, Shiva decreed that Ganapati should be invoked in prayer by one and all to ensure success. No act or prayer to any deity would succeed unless preceded by worship of Ganesha.

When Shiva set out to destroy the evil demon, Tripuraasura, he forgot his own ruling and rushed forth in great haste. However, as he got into his chariot, the nail in the wheel broke and the chariot could not be moved.

Amazed that such an event should have happened to him, Shiva stopped and pondered. He then realised that he had forgotten to pray to Ganesha and hence this impediment. He then invoked the name of his son and set out, achieving success in the Tripuraantaka war.

This story emphasises the importance of prayer to Ganesha at the beginning of every activity.

Ganesha worshipped by Vishnu

Another similar story concerns Vishnu.

As Bala Ganapati, the child Ganapati used to play with Shiva's *ganas* at the foot of Mount Kailas, the abode of Shiva and Parvati. Hiding in a flower garden, he would suck in water from the Ocean of Milk (on which Vishnu lay on his serpent Ananta) and spray it on the *ganas*, teasing them that it was raining.

Namasthe gajavakthraaya Herambaaya namonamah

Omkaaraakrithi roopaaya sagunaaya namonamah

(Mudgala Purana)

To the lord with the face of an elephant, also known as Heramba

To the one who is the embodiment of the symbol, OM, and is a part of the Saguna Brahman

18   *I bow to him again and again*

Vishnu one day found that his Valamburi Shankh (his sacred conch with swirls towards the right) was missing, and was perturbed. He then heard the deep resonant sound of a conch and knew that it was his Paanchajanya Shankh being blown in the vicinity of Mount Kailas. He now meditated on Shiva who said that anyone wishing to retrieve the conch should pray to Valamburi Ganesha (Ganesha in the rare posture of his trunk turned to the right). Vishnu did accordingly and Ganapati then returned the Paanchajanya Shankh to its rightful owner, Vishnu, who was overjoyed to have it back.

It is for this reason that when a Valamburi Ganesha image is found, it is believed to be very lucky for the owner.

Why Ganesha has a broken tusk

There are several legends as to how Ganesha broke one of his tusks, giving him the name, Ekadanta, the one with a single tusk.

The first pertains to his battle with Parashurama. Parashurama was one of the incarnations of Vishnu, born on earth to teach a lesson to the ruling classes, the Kshatriyas, who had become very arrogant and were riding rough-shod over the ordinary people. As a human on earth, he meditated on Shiva and obtained the divine axe, Parashu, with whose help he waged wars against all the erring princes and cleared the world of their evil.

Deeply indebted to Shiva, he then came to Mount Kailas to pay obeisance to his mentor. Ganesha, who was guarding the entrance to his fathers chambers, would not let him in, saying he had to wait till he obtained Shiva's permission. Parashurama felt that he, a devotee, needed no permission. When Ganesha refused to give in, Parashurama, hot-tempered at all times, struck Ganesha's tusk with his axe and broke it. Shiva and Parvati appeared before him and chastised Parashurama, who then worshipped Ganesha and obtained his forgiveness and blessings.

Ganesha's vehicle, the mouse

According to another legend, Ganesha broke his tusk himself in his war with Gajamukhaasura.

Gajamukha, a demon, did severe penance on the advice of Shukraachaarya, the guru of the *asuras* or demons, and obtained invincible powers from Shiva. He used these powers to harass the gods who then rushed to Ganesha for help. Ganesha battled with the demon but realised that, thanks to the powers given by Shiva, the evil one could not be killed.

Ganesha then broke his right tusk and threw it at Gajamukha cursing him to change into a mouse. He then got on to the back of the mouse and made it his vehicle, thereby keeping it under his control.

According to another Puranic story, Ganesha's rat was really the Gandharva, Krauncha. Once, in the court of Indra, the king of the Devas, Krauncha insulted the sage, Vaamadeva. He was then cursed by the latter and turned into a large rat.

The rat, true to its nature, entered the *ashram* of Sage Paraashara and caused great havoc to his dwelling as only a rat can. The Rishi then prayed to Vinayaka to save his simple dwelling. Ganesha appeared, made the rat his vehicle, and brought him under control.

As will be noticed, whatever the Puranic story, the purpose of making the rat his vehicle was to keep the rodent, whose nuisance value is high, under the control of Ganapati.

Ganesha, the scribe

The most interesting story concerning Ganesha is the belief that he was the scribe who wrote the Mahabharata. Sage Vyasa, the author of this epic, was advised by Brahma, on whom he meditated, to ask Ganesha to be the scribe to whom he could dictate the epic in verse form.

Ganapati appeared before Brahma and agreed to write, but on one condition, and that was that Vyasa would dictate continuously without pause. Vyasa agreed but he had his own condition, and that was that Ganesha should understand every word and thought and its implications before writing it down.

Whenever Vyasa found Ganesha had completed writing a verse, he would dictate a verse with very complex meanings so that Ganesha had to stop and think it over. This gave Vyasa time to compose a few stanzas mentally and dictate them when Ganesha was ready.

Ganesha used his broken tusk to write the Mahabharata, the longest epic the world has ever known. Is it surprising then that with Vyasa as the poet, Ganesha as the scribe and Krishna as the main hero, this epic has few equals in the world!

This story also has a lesson for mankind, that the Mahabharata should not be hurriedly read. It should be understood and digested, heard patiently and ruminated upon. In fact there is a superstition that the Mahabharata should never be read, only listened to, one small part at a time. Only then can one understand the depth of the meanings underlying the events in the epic.

Ganesha and the Moon

Once Ganesha partook of a huge meal of *modaka* (a sweet greatly favoured by him) and was riding home on his vehicle, the mouse. Suddenly the mouse was tripped by a snake. Ganesha fell off his back and his over-full stomach burst open and out tumbled the *modakas.*

Seeing this comic sight, Chandra, the Moon, burst into laughter. Ganesha got up, picked up the snake and tied it around his broken waist-line. (This snake-belt can be seen in many sculptures of Ganesha).

He then threw his broken tusk at the Moon and cursed him so that he would never again shine at night nor appear in the heavens. (In those times the full moon shone every day in the year).

Without the Moon, there was no night, no moonlight and no twilight. Young lovers moaned and wailed and the old groaned when they found they could not sleep in the bright sunlight which now shone even at night. The gods found life in the heavens as intolerable as human beings found the earth without the Moon.

The gods rushed to Ganesha and pleaded with him. The kind-hearted Ganesha relented but said that the Moon would no longer shine in full glory every night. He would wax and wane from a bright fortnight to a dark fortnight ending with the Full Moon and the New Moon alternately.

Also, it would not be lucky to see the Moon on Ganesh Chaturthi day (the fourth day of the bright fortnight) in the month of Bhaadrapad, as one who does will be the victim of scandal.

This superstition exists to this day, and people carefully avoid looking at the moon on Ganesh Chaturthi, the day of the festival of Ganesha. The over-superstitious however look downwards on Chaturthi day or the 4th day of the bright fortnight not only once a year but every month to be on the safe side!

Ganesha's wisdom

Shiva and Parvati were playing with their two sons, Ganesha and Kartikeya (or Murugan, as he is known to the Tamils). They had been given a fruit by the gods and both the sons wanted it. The divine couple explained to the sons that this fruit had in it the nectar of Supreme Knowledge and Immortality, and since both wanted it, the one who circled the world three times and came back first would get it as a prize. Kartikeya got on to his vehicle, the peacock, and flew into space, stopping at all sacred spots on the way and offering his prayers.

Ganesha knew that, with his corpulent form weighing him down, his vehicle, the mouse, would go even slower than usual and he could never beat Kartikeya.

But his wisdom taught him a solution. He walked round his parents, Shiva and Parvati, three times, with great devotion. When his parents asked him why he was not circling the globe, he answered — My parents, Shiva and Shakti are the whole world. Within them is the entire universe. I need go no further.

Naturally he won the fruit. This incident highlights the importance of intelligence, of which Ganesha is a repository, as against strength or speed or physical achievements.

Siddhi and Buddhi

The same story is altered in another Purana according to which Shiva and Parvati asked both their sons to race round the world thrice. The one to win would be married first.

Ganesha won by circumambulating his parents three times, who then married him to the daughters of Vishwaroopa, Siddhi (Achievement or Success) and Buddhi (Wisdom).

In most parts of India Vinayaka is considered a celibate but in some parts of the country he is considered married to these beautiful girls, a symbolic marriage to emphasise the importance of wisdom and success in removing obstacles.

Ganesha and Parvati

As a child, Ganesha teased a cat by pulling its tail, rolling it over on the ground and causing it great pain as naughty young boys are wont to do. After some time, tired of his game, he went to Kailas to his mother Parvati. He found her in great pain and covered with scratches and dust all over. When he questioned her, she put the blame on him. She explained that she was the cat whom Ganesha had teased.

This story is to teach us that all beings are part of divinity. Hurting one's fellow-creatures, human or animal, means hurting God himself just as Ganesha hurt Parvati by hurting the cat.

Ganesha learnt his lesson just as we need to do so here on earth.

Ganesha and the River Kaveri

To bring water to the arid areas of the South, Sage Agastya, with the blessings of Brahma, obtained water in his *kamandalu* (the vessel used to hold water for rituals of worship) from Shiva. He then came down south wanting to find the ideal spot from which the river could flow, and reached the Kodagu (Coorg) hills. He called out to a little boy (Ganesha in disguise), and asked him to hold the vessel carefully while he searched around for a good spot.

Ganesha, in his wisdom, selected the right place for the origin of the river, and left the *kamandalu* on the ground at the spot. A crow came and sat on the vessel and when Agastya returned and saw it, he shooed it away. When it flew off, it upset the *kamandalu* and the water gushing forth was the sacred River Kaveri flowing from the spot now known as Talakaveri.

Divinity manifests itself in many forms to help the people, and the benefits of the waters of the Kaveri are enjoyed to this day.

Ganesha and Ravana

Once the demon, Ravana, undertook the most difficult
tapasyas (austerities) and when Shiva appeared before him,
he asked as a boon that neither he nor his kingdom should
ever be destroyed or harmed.

Shiva then gave him a Shiva Lingam, the symbol of Shiva,
and said that he should take it to his kingdom and set it up
in a shrine with proper rituals. Only then would he become
invincible. But there was one condition — on no account
should the Lingam be placed on the ground as it would then
become immovable. Ravana was overjoyed and received
the Lingam.

However the lesser gods (Devas) were frightened with the
consequences of Ravana obtaining all this power, and
prayed to Ganesha.

Varuna, the god of the waters, entered Ravana's abdomen
forcing him to stop en route. Desperately, not wanting to
keep the Lingam down, Ravana hailed a young boy who was
passing by and asked him to hold on to the stone Lingam
for a few minutes. Ravana had barely left when the boy
called out to him thrice and when there was no reply,
kept the Lingam on the ground. When Ravana returned, he
was furious and chased the boy, threatening to kill him.

The boy took his true form as Ganesha, and over-powering Ravana, rolled him into a ball and threw him into the sky and played with him. Ravana realised his limitations and also as to how all-powerful Ganesha was.

This spot where the Lingam was placed by Ganesha is Gokarna on the west coast of Karnataka. It is worshipped to this day.

This story teaches the lesson that evil ultimately loses, especially when it aspires for power.

Ganesha and Kubera

Kubera, the god of wealth, was proud of his endless riches and hosted a lavish dinner which the child Ganesha attended.

Once Ganesha started to eat, no one else had anything left for himself. After wiping clean the food laid out, Ganesha started to eat the vessels, the furniture and all of Alakaapuri, Kubera's capital.

When nothing was left, the child threatened to swallow Kubera himself who then ran and fell at the feet of Shiva, asking for his help, as Ganesha's voracious hunger had no limit.

Shiva then gave Ganesha a handful of roasted grain, which he ate, and immediately his hunger was appeased.

This teaches the lesson that a handful of puffed rice given with love and eaten with devotion is more important and filling than all the wealth of Kubera flaunted to impress the gods.

Why Ganesha has stayed single

Often it is asked why Ganesha, beloved of the gods and of all humanity, remained a Brahmachari, single and celibate (as believed in the South).

A legend states that the reason was that he felt that his mother, Parvati, was the most beautiful and perfect woman in the universe. Bring me a woman as beautiful as she is, and I shall marry her, he said.

None could find an equal to the lovely Uma. The gods are still searching, and so is Ganesha!

Namasthe vighnamaayaaya namasthe sarva saakshinay

Sarvaathmanay svayam vedya roopinay thay namo namah

(Mudgala Purana)

I bow to him who is part of the illusion of obstacles

Who is the witness of all that is happening in the world

Who is the Atman of all

To him who knows and understands himself and his form, I bow in obeisance

30 Vishwaroopa Ganapati, Tanjore painting

We have, so far, studied the birth and importance of Ganesha as given in Puranic legends and religious lore. We shall now examine the origin of Ganesha as evidenced in art and archaeology from the earliest times.

As we have seen, the legends referring to the origin of Ganesha are many and often highly contradictory. Most of them appear in Sanskrit literature of just a thousand years ago or even later. This has given rise to a commonly held belief that Ganesha appears very late in Indian art also.

Archaeological finds have however disproved this theory. While it is true that in the early period he appears only as a Vyantara Devata or minor god, the fact is that, even in this form, he appears fairly early in both art and literature. Also, astonishingly, many of the late legends describe some of the earliest forms of the deity as evidenced in archaeological finds. Thus the memory of man and oral traditions are often as old as the earliest forms of Ganesha.

The earliest literary references to Ganapati as the Lord of the *ganas* are in connection with deities other than himself. Brihaspati is addressed as *ganaanaam tvaa ganapatim havaamahe* (Rig Veda). However, as in several other cases, the description is transferred to Indra on another occasion when he is also addressed as Ganapati.

The Taittiriya Aranyaka refers to Dantin, who has a twisted trunk *(vaktratunda)* and who holds a sheaf of corn, a sugarcane and a club.

In later literature, the *ganas* are short, hardy spirits, a sort of Yaksha, and the Lord of the Ganas could mean the Lord of the hosts of spirits, many malevolent. As their lord, he kept them in check, a quality that was to be integrated into a later form of Ganesha, Vighneshwara, the Lord of obstacles, preventing malevolent spirits from harming one's efforts.

It is unlikely that the Ganapati of the Rig Veda was the elephant-headed god. Firstly, there is no reference in the Rig Veda to the elephant, which is too large an animal to miss. Secondly, Brihaspati and Indra are referred to as Ganapati in the sense of "Lord of the Ganas".

The root *gana* means to count or to list and Ganapati could mean the lord of the countless ones, either an epithet for the countless spirits inherent in the material world or the Devas themselves.

His major role in Indian literature is as the scribe of the Mahabharata. According to belief, Vyasa prayed to Brahma who advised him to ask Ganapati to write the epic. (See chapter on Puranic Lore).

Ganesha, Gupta 4th *c.*
Udayagiri, M.P.

It is interesting that this late legend, and perhaps its even later interpolation in the epic, is the earliest form of the elephant-headed god as we know him.

Excavations carried out in Luristan (Western Iran) revealed a plaque containing an elephant-headed figure. Dressed as a warrior, he holds a sword and snake in one hand, a quill in another. The trident is to one side and at his feet is a snake. The figure also appears to be bearded, a sign of great wisdom (as in the *rishis* of India, the *magi* of Persia, etc.). The quill too was a symbol of learning and knowledge.

This plaque has been dated to between 1200 and 1000 B.C., corresponding to the later Vedic period in India, just preceding the period of the Taittiriya Aranyaka cited earlier. This also corresponds to the approximate date of the Mahabharata War.

Early religions being generally based on nature worship, they gave traits of character and characteristics to plants and animals, finding within them spirits of good or evil. The large but gentle elephant was the embodiment of goodness and virtue, his size belying his non-violent nature. Thus did the elephant-headed one become the repository of wisdom, for it could only have been wisdom that made him abhor physical violence which, given his size, would have made him an object of fear.

The existence of animism is apparent from Harappan seals. However, in most cases, the body is that of an animal with a human head. The elephant too figures in this form. There are other figures of a more complex form, combining between two or four animals with a human form or face. One such figure combines four — the fore-legs of an ox, the feet of a tiger, the horns of a bull (or antelope) and the trunk and tusks of an elephant. We have no knowledge of who it could be but, interestingly, the resemblance to the *ganas* or attendants of Shiva is remarkable.

But the inherent fear invoked by the massive mammal could not be ignored, and another aspect emerged, that of the Vinayaka or malignant beings who created obstacles and difficulties (Aitareya Brahmana). This too was a characteristic of the elephant.

It was but natural that ancient people, who deified all nature, would worship nature's greatest creation on land. By this time food gatherers had changed to food producers and therefore required just that skill which the elephant displayed. They were no longer aggressive hunters, yet they required superior strength to survive against all obstacles. They needed the wisdom and judgement displayed by the elephant to know what to do when.

The adoption of the elephant for its intrinsic qualities is undoubtedly a facet of totemism, by which clans or families selected an animal or bird as their symbol and deified it, in this case the elephant. If its role was symbolic of qualities

Plaque from Luristan, Western Iran

33

Ganapati of the Nagas

which the tribe wished to acquire from their propitiation of the god, who were the original worshippers of Ganapati?

The Vedic Aryans were, themselves, nomadic tribes who could have propitiated the elephant, as the epithet Dantin indicates. The Taittiriya Aranyaka reference also emphasizes the elephant's penchant for agricultural produce — the sheaf of corn and the sugarcane — which it shares with man. It was obviously a food-producing society.

The Luristan plaque displays the elephant-headed one's ability to write. This too reflects a settled, advanced society which had mastered the art of writing.

The Taittiriya Aranyaka had also described Dantin as holding a club. The club is a Neolithic weapon used by people in that transitional phase of society.

However there is one major flaw in the theory of a Vedic origin of Ganesha, and that is the elephant head. The Vedic religion is a celebration of Nature, an Indian pantheism revelling in the sheer beauty and unpredictability of the elements. But Nature, for the Vedic people, was the sun and the rain, the wind, the waters and the stars. There is little or no veneration of animals, although some are mentioned. Even the cow is cherished for her economic value rather than for her qualities. It is thus most unlikely that Dantin originated with the Vedic Aryans.

On the other hand, the history of the indigenous peoples of India is replete with instances of animal and tree worship. The Nagas and the *peepul* (bo) tree are, after Ganesha, the most popular. Every tribe had its totem, and non-Vedic deities, like Kartikeya and Devi, are invariably associated with animals (the peacock and lion respectively, in this case), unlike the Vedic Indra and Varuna who were given animal vehicles much later. Dantin himself appears only in the Taittiriya Aranyaka, compiled long after the Rig Veda, the earliest work. By this time, non-Vedic deities had crept into the Rig Veda, and Ganesha was one such instance.

34   Harappan Seal

Ganesha from Kantaka Cetinga Stupa, Sri Lanka

Mathura Ganapati, 5th *c.*   35

The name Dantin is probably the original Sanskrit name of the deity. Words like *pallu* and *pella* in Dravidian languages signify teeth. The Tamil name for Ganesha, Pillaiyar, has come to mean the "noble child" *(pillai = child)*, but this is a much later development. The earlier meaning was obviously the tusked one from Pallu or Dantin. In Pali, *pillaka* meant a young elephant.

The *ganas* were soon identified with the countless spirits that roamed the nether world, spirits whose non-Vedic origins cannot be in doubt, as they are totally alien to the Vedic world. As a rotund, elephant-headed figure, Dantin became their lord and master, and thus became Ganapati.

His *vakra tunda*, or twisted trunk, is a little more perplexing, for there is no appropriate reason to account for it. Perhaps it was the elephant's own ability to grossly twist his trunk into odd shapes that earned him this epithet.

There are differing legends on how Ganesha broke his tusk himself or had it broken (see chapter on Puranic lore), and used it as a weapon.

Ivory charms were very popular, believed to ward off the evil eye and other unpopular obstacles. The loss of one tusk probably signifies the passing of the luck to the devotee in the form of an ivory charm.

The tusk is also club-like in its utilisation, when thrown at the enemy. However, none of these stories are sufficient explanations for the single-tusked character, given the fact that a single tusk denotes a physical aberration which is anathema to Hindu canons of iconography.

The single tusk could also have agricultural associations in its resemblance to the plough. This association is reinforced by Ganesha's agricultural attributes, the sugarcane and corn and, later, the *modaka*, a sweet offering of the harvest.

Ganesha was, obviously, a god of the harvest, particularly of sugarcane growers, for he both carries the plant and a sweet produced from it. This takes us nearer the origins of the god, for sugarcane was and still is grown in the Deccan and Southern India. The earliest Ganeshas too are found in this region and, till today, Ganesha occupies pride of place among the people of these areas.

The farmer's greatest enemy, then and now, is the mouse or rat. In pre-rat poison days, the elephant alone had the ability to destroy them en masse, by trampling on them with his big feet. This was yet another reason for Ganesha's veneration by the agriculturist. His role in the destruction of the rat may have been celebrated by the huge elephant-headed figure sitting incongruously on the tiny *mooshika* or mouse. The contrast is startling, but it is intended. Here was the superman establishing his authority over the pest, much as Shiva dances his *tandava* over the squirming *asura* or demon. This is further reinforced by the fact that, unlike Shiva's vehicle Nandi or Vishnu's vehicle Garuda who are,

themselves, objects of veneration, Ganesha's mouse-vehicle is never propitiated with the god or separately. At best he is ignored. The fact that the rat only appears in Western and Southern images where he is a harvest deity is reinforced by the fact that in Kashmir and the Western Himalayas, the rat does not appear with figures of the god.

A thirteenth century Nepalese miniature painting in the Pingalamala, in the Nepal State Library, shows Ganesha seated cross-legged on the rat with his broken tusk in his right hand, pointing downwards as if it were a pen. However it is unlikely that the tusk originated as a stylus, for the elephant-headed scribe of the Luristan plate uses a quill pen.

The legends of Ganesha suggest that the broken tusk was a weapon of the god. Parasurama's axe cuts it off, in a

Ganesha, Gupta 5th *c.*
Bhumara, M.P.
Indian Museum, Calcutta

37

Ganesha, Bikkavolu, A.P.
38 Eastern Chalukya, 7th *c.*

weapon-to-weapon encounter, or Ganesha breaks it off himself to aim it at the moon, or at the demon, Gajamukhaasura, as a sort of missile.

The single tusk obviously had several connotations, as a club-like weapon, stylus and plough. Coupled to these were the folk use of ivory charms, particularly among Tantrics.

Interestingly, the Nepalese manuscript mentioned earlier is Tantric, dictated by Shiva to his son Ganesha. Ganesha in turn uses his ivory tusk as his pen.

The early Ganesha figures are all found in the Deccan, where sugarcane grows in abundance. Furthermore, the early Ganeshas were invariably found with the Saptamatrika or seven mothers, who were fertility goddesses propitiated to ensure a good harvest and many children. Obviously then, Ganesha was a fertility deity of a Deccan people. This is further reinforced by the fact that Ganesha appears very late in the north. He is missing in the coins and seals of the Kushana period, a notable omission, for Hindu iconography received a major growth impetus at this time. His earliest known appearance in northern India is in the pre-Gupta and Gupta periods — an era which saw a major syncretism of cults into Hinduism. It is to this genre that Ganesha belonged.

At the foot of the elephant-headed scribe of the Luristan plate, there is a snake. Tantric texts too describe Ganapati as holding a snake. Interestingly, the Satapatha Brahmana often uses the term Naga to describe the elephant. Ganesha, with a five-hooded Naga canopy, is worshipped by several esoteric sects. Many of his images portray the snake coiled around his stomach or neck, or as a sacred thread over his left shoulder, while in some statues from Nepal he holds the snake in both arms.

Folk and primitive images of Ganapati, particularly those found under trees or in the open, are often accompanied by Naga stones on which inter-coiling snakes are carved. In several primitive images of Ganesha, the snake spreads its hood over the deity. In the art of both Ellora (in Maharashtra) and Burma, Ganesha is associated with the crocodile, a symbol of the Makaras, a Naga tribe.

The snake has been a constant presence in the iconography of Ganesha, particularly in the earlier periods, and is probably the missing link. The Nagas were a powerful ancient non-Vedic people who once ruled over most of India. That they were totemic is without doubt, for in early Buddhist art (as at Barhut), the Naga devotees of the Buddha are distinguished by the multi-hooded snake canopy over their heads.

The Nagas had known sub-divisions, such as the Garudis (Garuda worshippers) and Makaras. They were animists who worshipped spirits of trees and animals, as is evidenced by the inevitable association of the Naga or snake stones, in

Ganesha with Tandava Shiva
Badami, Karnataka

most of Southern India, with the *peepul* tree. This form of worship embraced the vast multitude of Yakshas and Ganas, spirits of nature venerated by the primitive peoples.

It appears then that the Gajas were a sub-sect of the Nagas. Their god was the elephant-headed Ganesha. The Yakshas and Ganas, who formed a part of this religion, gave him their characteristics — short, pot-bellied and large-headed, a grotesque body yet a lovable soul. He was their leader, Ganapati.

In a decorative first or second century A.D. frieze around the Kantaka Cetinga Stupa, near Mihintale in Sri Lanka, a double procession of ganas converges towards a central dwarfish elephant-headed figure whose trunk is turned to the left. This is, undoubtedly, Ganapati.

The Vinayakas often appear in Sanskrit literature as *ganas* or tribes. Vinayaka, too, is a name of Ganesha. Their unacceptability to the official religion is indicated by the fact that they are often described as malevolent or even just as pesky nuisances.

The Yajnavalkya Smriti describes the Vinayakas as spirits to be propitiated who would otherwise possess men and women, make them failures and put obstacles in their performance of good deeds. The Mahabharata and the Grihyasutras also describe them as imps and evil spirits. Ganapati, the Vinayaka, was Vighnaraja as the king of obstacles, Vighnanaashin as the destroyer of obstacles, and Siddhidaata as the giver of success. Thus the malevolent Vinayaka became the remover of obstacles himself. To this was added the Vedic title, Ganapati, or lord of the *ganas*. All the various characteristics had coalesced.

While the scribe is mentioned late in Sanskrit literature, it must not be forgotten that the ability to write is one of the earliest traits of the elephant-headed god.

Writing denotes education and knowledge, particularly in the beginnings of civilisation. Scribes or literates were always the upper class in any society, on the top-most bracket of the intelligentsia, be it in Egypt, Babylon or India. The worshippers of the elephant-headed scribe were obviously an upper class, who venerated knowledge and wisdom over more mundane or violent qualities.

The Nagas too had their caste system. The Garudis and Makaras were superior castes of Nagas, as their mythology indicates, for the Nagas are always defeated by them or are found serving them. This distinction still continues among the Garudis in Andhra Pradesh, where the Garuda worshippers are considered superior to the Naga worshippers, and the two will not inter-marry.

It is likely therefore that the elephant-worshippers represented the upper echelon of the Nagas, a class which could read and write and claimed the wisdom of the wise and powerful elephant as their own.

Bhumara Ganesha and Shakti
Boston Museum of Fine Arts

In the syncretism of different Indian religious cults, Ganesha, the elephant-headed one, was invested with a mythology to explain the head to a non-animal worshipping people, and a father and mother in Shiva and Parvati.

That he was the god of the obviously more powerful upper classes among the Nagas is reinforced by the fact that, whereas his cult and worship remained independent and he was revered for his own qualities, the lesser status of the worshippers of Garuda, Makara and the vast body of Nagas or snake worshippers relegated their totemic symbols to obscurity. Among themselves their status is visible: the Garudis were superior to the Makaras and Nagas, so their symbol became the vehicle of Vishnu. The Makaras went into obscurity, while the snake god of the Nagas, because of the sheer numbers and geographic spread of his worshippers, hovered between two roles, one as the bed (and support) of Vishnu, around the neck of Shiva or the waist of Ganesha, and another as a deity on the fringes of society worshipped in groves and open fields outside cities in the form of Naga stones.

The sequence of events is probably thus — the elephant-headed deity, god of the upper classes among the Nagas, and propitiated as a scribe and as a protector of the harvest, entered the Hindu pantheon as a full god with a cult and following of his own.

It is also interesting that the rise in popularity of Ganesha along with Shiva and Vishnu coincides with the decline of Buddhism and, with it, the many Yakshas and Yakshis who were associated with Buddhism. It is likely that the absorption of the elephant-headed god, among others, whose popularity was wide among certain indigenous tribes, hastened the decline of dependence on a host of nature spirits associated with Buddhism and, thereby, Vighneshwara as their lord, Ganapati, subdued them to the growth of his personality and cult.

The importance of Ganapati in the post-Buddhist Hindu renaissance is affirmed by the fact that Mahayana Buddhism believed that the *Ganapati hridaya mantra* was taught to Ananda by the Buddha himself. The worship of Ganapati travelled with Mahayana Buddhism to South-East Asia, Tibet, China, Central Asia, Mongolia and Japan. In fact, the conversion of Mongolia to Buddhism is credited to this god. The Tibetan saint and missionary, P'ags-pa, narrates how, before his birth, his father invoked Ganesha, who, appearing before him, carried him on his trunk to Mount Meru and showed him Mongolia as the land to be conquered by his unborn son. It was P'ags-pa who converted Kublai Khan, the Chinese emperor, in the 13th century, and spread Mahayana Buddhism to Mongolia.

The Yajnavalkya Samhita mentions that a Vinayaka was the son of Ambika. This text does not identify Vinayaka with the elephant-headed deity, but this was done later. This identification was the beginning of a confused mythology about the origin of Ganesha, his elephant head, and his association with Shiva and Parvati, a mythology required for integrating him with the official religion.

To sum up, the elephant-headed god, worshipped as a scribe and as a harvest deity, was the deity of a non-Vedic people, the Nagas. He combined within him the qualities of the elephant, strength and wisdom, and the qualities of the spirits of the other world. As the Lord of the wise, he was their scribe. As the Lord of the farmers, he protected their fields from rats and ensured a good harvest.

His earliest *avatar* was as a scribe of the Naga tribes, a quality that is to be recalled much later. Somewhere in the course of Indian history, his worship moved southwards to the Deccan plateau, where the farmers, particularly the sugarcane growers, venerated him for a good harvest. His destruction of their enemy, the rat, gave the rodent a position beneath him or his foot. To satisfy the elephant's sweet tooth, his devotees gave him the sugarcane in one hand and a sweet in another.

The chequered development of the elephant-headed one, Dantin or Ganapati, was to be reflected in the changing icon of the god. In the absence of a written narrative, the icon alone can trace his origin till historical times. By the Gupta period, an age of Hindu renaissance and consolidation, the integration of his various associations was complete and his cult popular enough to make Adi Shankara, three centuries later, list Ganapatya or the cult of Ganapati as one of the Shanmata or six paths of the Hindu faith.

Ganapati had now become one of the major gods of popular Hinduism.

Ganesha, Pandrethan, Kashmir, 7th *c.*

Black stone Ganesha
Bengal, 11th *c.*

44

Ganesha is a treasure-house of knowledge for the iconologist. The evolution of his icon is a case study of the role of iconographic development itself. All this is in spite of the fact that the most important feature, the elephant head, has remained constant and unchanging.

A Harappan seal contains an elephant-headed composite image. The face is tilted to a side in a half to three-quarter view, with the trunk flowing to the right as in later Indian art.

The next elephant-headed figure is to be seen in the Luristan plate mentioned earlier. The figure holds a quill in one hand and a snake slithers at his feet. Neither are described as Ganapati, but both are undoubtedly proto-types.

On an Amaravati coping, there is a pot-bellied, elephant-headed figure below a long garland held up by Ganas. It has been described as a Yaksha, but there is no reason why it should not be a proto-type of Ganapati, if not Ganesha himself.

The image of Ganesha is, undoubtedly, Yaksha in conception — short, pot-bellied, large-headed, and often awkward. Yet, like the imps of the Indian nether world, Ganapati can be spry, animated and lovable, a veritable Puck of Hindu mythology.

His attributes were, according to the Taittiriya Aranyaka, a sheaf of corn, sugarcane and a club. Later, these change to an axe (*parashu)* and *moolaka* (radish) or a bulbous root eaten by an elephant. They may also be an *ankusha* (elephant goad), *paasha* (noose), *naga* (snake) and *modaka* (the sweet dish he is associated with). All these, in various ways, illustrate the character of the god, as either a harvest deity or, more often, as just an elephant.

Other characteristics are his three eyes (a Shaivite association) and the *vyalayajnopavita* (sacred thread made of the serpent, a Naga association). He may also hold a *kapiththa* (wood apple), his own tusk, rosary, lotus, etc. The peculiar *Ekadanta* (single tooth or tusk) is another iconographic feature peculiar to Ganesha and has yet to be satisfactorily explained.

The early figures of the god are two-armed. If the identity of the Amaravati figure is in any doubt, that of the single-tusked elephant-headed figure, flanked by ganas, on a frieze of the Kantaka Cetinga Stupa, near Mihintale in Sri Lanka, is undoubtedly the elephant-headed god. The *stupa* is referred to in inscriptions of the first and second centuries.

A twenty-inch high two-armed bas-relief from Mathura consists of an over-sized head and ears, a nude torso that is short, with skinny, awkward limbs. The bent right arm holds a pointed object, probably a tusk. The left arm holds a bowl, while the deity's trunk coils to the left and dips into the bowl. The object in the right hand is not clear, but the pointed top indicates that it must have been the broken tusk. This figure may be ascribed to the 2nd century A.D. and is probably the earliest known sculpture of Ganesha on his own, perhaps used as an object of veneration.

This standing Ganesha is very similar to an early Gupta image from Udayagiri (Bhilsa, Madhya Pradesh). Seated in the *ardhaparyanka* posture, his trunk (now broken) turns left to dip into the cup held in his left hand. The heads of both the figures are very similar — wide foreheads, with barely separated ears, short or practically no necks on short bodies with skinny arms. The mouse is also missing in both cases. There is a suggestion of *yajnopavita* (sacred thread) in both (the figures are very indistinct), although there is nothing to suggest the snake.

In a 5th century A.D. figure from Bhumara in Madhya Pradesh, Ganesha wears a *yajnopavita* of bells, with bells on the head-dress, bracelets and anklets. Coomaraswamy has described it as a Yaksha who was probably the temple doorkeeper. However it is more likely to represent the practice of adorning the temple elephant with bells. The tradition of decorating Ganesha figures with bells, to substitute for the bells of an elephant, was and still is a tradition in Tamil Nadu.

A slightly later statue from Bhumara is the earliest representation of Shakti Ganesha. He holds an axe and a goad in his upper right and left hands respectively, and the broken tusk in the lower right. His left arm is around Shakti seated on his lap. He is very simply adorned, in contrast to the bejewelled goddess, with a snake as a waist-belt. His trunk dips into a bowl held by the goddess.

Ganesha's status varies from bachelorhood to married to bigamous, the first being a firmly entrenched southern tradition, while the last appears to be a later personification of his wisdom and achievement in Siddhi and Buddhi. But the Shakti Ganeshas are a class apart, and possibly have Tantric associations. As every deity receives his *shakti*

Ganesha with Shiva and Saptamatrika
Aihole, Karnataka, 8th *c.*

Ganesha with Hariti and Vasudhare

(power) from the female principle, so does Ganesha. This is reinforced by the fact that, in the Bhumara figure, the earliest of its kind, all the three attributes held by the god are weapons. There is no sweet in Ganesha's hand, an inevitable association of the deity. The bowl of sweet or fruit is held by his Shakti, and his trunk dips into it. In this is the bowl of elixir which gives him super-human strength. It is worth recalling that Tantricism with its emphasis on sex as part of religion, was very popular at this period.

In all the early figures it is interesting to note that the trunk is always dipping into a bowl held on the left by Ganesha or his Shakti.

While in figures mentioned above, Ganesha is invariably independent and free-standing, in the Deccan figures hereafter, he is invariably found in association with the Saptamatrika (seven mother goddesses) or other deities. This is interesting because it was both in this region and at this period that his worship was gaining popularity.

The only image of Ganapati at the 6th century cave temple at Badami is at the foot of an enormous bas-relief of Shiva dancing'the *tandava*. Ganesha's divinity is confirmed by the halo behind his head. Carried away by the Rudra *tandava*, Ganesha too dances, making this the earliest dancing figure of the god. He is four-armed, but two are broken. One left arm holds a bowl, a visible right follows Shiva's movement.

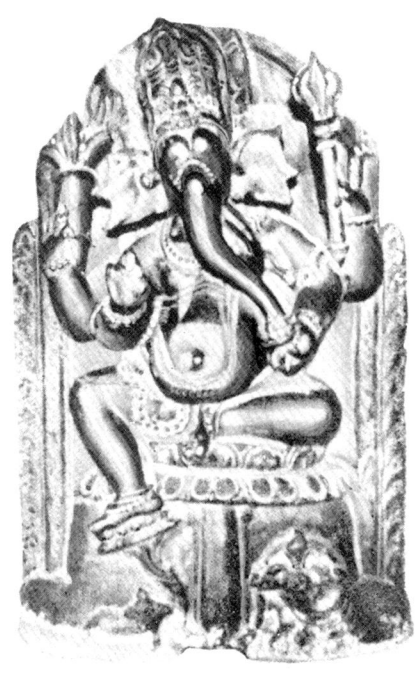

Ganesha holding radish, Bangladesh

47

Saatvika Vinayaka
48 Tanjore Painting, early 19th *c.*

He similarly attends Shiva's *tandava* in the rock-cut Chalukyan temples at Aihole.

The association of the Saptamatrika with Ganesha may be seen in the Galaganath Temple at Aihole in Karnataka. Each Matrika has her *vahana* (vehicle) beneath her throne to identify her. Ganesha has a mouse. Ganesha is distinctively shorter than the Matrikas, although his *asana* (throne) is on level with theirs.

It is in Ellora in Maharashtra that Ganesha appears in very different and peculiar situations.

In the 6th century Vakataka Rameshwara Cave, and at Kailasa, he appears again with the haloed Seven Mothers. As at Aihole, each has her *vahana* below, Ganesha's being damaged. Shiva is seated to the right of the Matrikas, Ganesha to the left. In this composition Ganesha is slightly larger than the Matrikas, indicating his growing importance.

This method of representation was not unique. In the Vakataka Cave III at Aurangabad, there is a panel of seven haloed female devotees with a haloed standing Buddha to the left, similar to the Matrika composition. In the Vakataka Cave XII at Ellora there are seven haloed Buddhas. Obviously, there was a popular belief in seven similar figures which were represented variously. This format is adapted in later art. In an 11th century Pala composition, the Seven Mothers are replaced by the Navagraha (nine planets) in anthropomorphic form, with Ganesha at the right end. The representations of Ganesha with the Navagrahas appears in South India, Orissa and Bengal.

In the Rashtrakuta Cave, Ravan-ka-khai, the Saptamatrika sit on thrones under which is the vehicle identifying each mother. Ganesha is the eighth, with a bowl of sweets under his throne.

In an unique composition in the Lankeshvara Cave, Parvati stands between two fires. She is four-armed, her upper left holding a small figure of Ganesha and her upper right a Shiva *linga.* At her feet is the crocodile or *makara,* symbolic of the river Ganga.

Interestingly, the Makaras were a Naga tribe. This association of the *makara* and Ganesha was to reappear in Burmese images of the god.

Ganesha appears in several other scenes of the *tandava* and other incidents of Shiva's legends. However he is a small figure in a large tableau, as in the scene of the marriage of Shiva and Parvati at Ellora. Ganesha is generally four-armed, with a combination of attributes mentioned earlier. The *modaka* (sweet) is invariably present, the mouse occasionally. At Elephanta, he is surrounded by his *ganas.*

The association of Ganesha with Shiva and Parvati had been established in the Chalukyan and Vakataka periods, but

Bronze Ganesha
Tiruottiyur, Tamil Nadu

49

this was as a part of a tableau, where Ganesha is a spectator or participant, however active. There is no indication of his status as their son. Ganesha is still a Vyantara Devata, a minor deity. Even the Pallavas omitted Ganesha from their temples of Somaskanda — Shiva and Parvati with the child Skanda — of which there are two in the Shore Temples at Mamallapuram, But while there are seated, standing and even dancing Ganeshas, he is never a part of the family scene, and is conspicuous by his absence.

Ganesha as the son of Shiva and Parvati makes his appearance in the Deccan again. In the ninth century Eastern Chalukyan Golingeshwara Temple at Bikkavolu in Andhra Pradesh, there is a sculpture of Shiva and Parvati as Alingana Chandrashekaramurti and a seated Ganesha. Although the temple and even Shiva and Parvati betray strong Pallava influences, Ganesha wears a northern crown, a garland of bells on his neck and feet, a stomach band and a snake as the sacred thread. One hand holds a rosary, another an axe, the third the broken tusk, and the fourth the vessel of sweets.

All of Ganesha's four arms are generally utilised in these early figures. Rarely is one left free for the *abhaya mudra* as in the case of other gods.

On a column dated A.D. 862 at Ghatiyala near Jodhpur, there is an inscription praising Ganesha. Four images of the deity are placed back to back of the top column, facing the four cardinal points, reminiscent of the four elephants or *dig-gajas* supporting the heavens.

The eighth century and thereafter saw variations of the Ganesha icon and its growth in size and importance. From a small figure attending Shiva or the Matrikas, he has a separate niche or even a shrine for himself, particularly in South Indian temples. His stature has grown, particularly in the Deccan and South India where Ganesha now has a temple in every village.

Different regions preferred different variations of the god. Most southern temples enshrine a seated Ganesha, comfortably accepting his devotees' offerings and obeisance. The four hands hold one or more of his popular attributes — the noose, goad, axe, tusk and sweet.

In Southern India Ganesha images played several roles, from the chief deity of a village to another as watchman, under *peepul* trees and beside snake stones. His role as the dispeller of obstacles made his worship precede prayer to any other deity. For such a temporary role, he could be represented by a block of stone with some ambivalent features painted on it. Even today, in the domestic or village worship of another deity, the preceding prayer to Ganesha restricts the god to a small pyramid of turmeric powder mixed with water or to a mound of clay.

The radish was popular in Bengal and Nepal, where it was obviously a local variation. Nepal was also the home of the

Punchamukha Vinayaka
Bronze image

50

Dancing Ganesha
Gangaikondacholapuram, Tamil Nadu   51

many-armed (from six to twelve) Ganeshas, Heramba of the five heads, (often accompanied by Shakti and/or seated on a lion), Shakti Ganesha and other esoteric forms. These Ganeshas are generally fierce-looking and violent, brandishing their weapons. Later, the Shakti of Ganesha manifests herself as Ganeshini, particularly in Central India and the Deccan.

In the *Sadyojata* Mother and child sculptures of Bengal, Parvati (the mother) reclines with a child beside her. Ganesha and Kartikeya are invariably also present, indicating that neither was identified with the child. In this case the child was probably Shiva, from the Puranic account of the *swayamvara* of Parvati, the daughter of Himavaan. To test her, Shiva took the form of a new-born child and was found on her lap. Parvati, through her meditation, recognised the child to be Shiva.

A very popular and iconographically attractive form through various periods of Indian art has been Nritya Ganapati, the dancing Ganesha. First appearing in the early Chalukyan sculpture, his dance loses its gay abandon in Chola sculpture, but gains in sophistication and aesthetics. Thereafter, the four-armed Ganesha becomes two, six, eight, ten or twelve-armed in the various schools of art.

Ganesha, 5th *c.*
Samalaji, Gujarat
52 Baroda Museum

Sometimes one arm is thrown across the body as in the Rudra *tandava,* at other times it is raised in a *mudra* or holds a rosary. Generally, one foot is merely raised off the ground, as the short rotund body could barely balance on one foot and cross the other across the body.

Some of the most beautiful dancing Ganeshas are from Orissa, where a wealth of detail and decoration accompany graceful body movements, sometimes even in *tribhanga* (three bends), in comparison to the more statuesque Chola Nritya Ganapatis. In Nepal, Tantricism converts the happy dancing figure into a violent twelve-armed, five-headed god standing in the vortex of a tumultuous happening, surrounded by so many more dancing Ganeshas, each with one leg raised in *ardha padmaasana* and the other planted on a grimacing rat or lion. The Nepalese figure is red here, with a radish replacing the broken tusk and a *chintamani* (jewel) replacing the sweet.

The development of these forms owes its origin either to the Vaamaachara Tantric cults (as in the case of Shakti Ganesha, Unmatta Vinayaka and Ucchishta Ganapati) or to the development of Puranic legends, coinciding with the absorption of Ganesha into the Shaivite fold and, thereby, mainstream Hinduism. With the inclusion of Shakti came the lion as yet another mount for Ganesha. However the lion is generally found only in northern Tantric images and rarely, if ever, in the Deccan and the south.

An enormous seventh century Ganesha from Pandrethan in Kashmir sits on a throne supported by two crouching lions. The figure is badly damaged, but the trunk curving to the left and dipping into the bowl of sweets is visible.

The rat never appears in Kashmiri or Himalayan sculpture, where the lion is invariably his vehicle. As the lion is the vehicle of Durga or Shakti, this association obviously came in with Tantricism.

It is in the Rajput and Pahadi paintings that Ganesha finally finds his family, Shiva, Parvati and his brother Kartikeya. The four form several happy tableaux with the adoring parents lovingly fondling the two young boys.

By the eighth-ninth centuries, the *shastras* had begun to be compiled and various texts after this period describe the various iconographic forms, which range from eight to sixteen to thirty-two, depending on the *dhyana shloka.* By the end of the medieval period they had been consolidated and were, henceforth, the guide of every sculptor and temple builder.

Ganesha with Shakti
Madurai, Tamil Nadu

Ganesha, Chedi, M.P.

53

54   Stone Ganesha from Java, 10th *c.*

Ganesha was one of the many Hindu deities to traverse Asia along with Buddhism. However his earliest appearance in Afghanistan was as the Hindu Maha Vinayaka. On a sculpture found at Gardez and later removed to the Dargah Pir Rattan Nath at Kabul where it is worshipped by local Hindus, is an inscription saying:

> *This great and beautiful Maha Vinayaka was consecrated by the renowned Shahi King, the illustrious Shahi khingala.*

The figure is made of marble, 60 cms high and 35 cms wide. Both stylistically and paleographically, the figure belongs to the early 6th century A.D. The four arms are broken, but the traces of the broken tusk and a left-turning trunk linger. The god's *yajnopavita* ends in a knot simulating a snake's hood. What is remarkable about this image is the strong Gandharan influence, from the flat coronet on his head to his casual stance.

An undated but probably earlier figure belongs to Sakar Dhar (formerly Shankar Dhar), north of Kabul, and is now worshipped by the Hindus at Narsingdwara in Kabul. As in the other figure, he wears a *yajnopavita* ending in a knot shaped like a snake's hood. His right tusk is whole, the left is broken. Obviously, this is the Ekadanta form. His ears bulge out like two fans. His upper arms are missing, but the lower two rest on two curly-haired ganas reminiscent of the *ayudha purushas* of the Gupta temples of Deogarh. The very Gupta appearance of these two suggest that the figure itself belongs to the 4th century, making it one of the earliest Ganeshas still worshipped today.

Ganesha was equally popular in Buddhism, particularly the Mahayana school, and, as stated earlier, the Ganapati *hridaya mantra* was believed to have been disclosed to Ananda by the Buddha himself, according to Nepalese traditions.

However, the earliest known appearance of Ganesha in Buddhist art, apart from the Amaravati coping and Kantaka Cetinga Stupa figures mentioned earlier, where he appears to be a mere Yaksha or Gana, is in a late Gupta frieze from Sarnath, accompanied by other Brahmanic deities at the *parinirvana* of the Buddha.

Later, particularly in Tibet and occasionally in Nepal, he appears as a malevolent demon, Vinayaka.

But these are aberrations, as an early Nepalese legend says that Ashoka's daughter, Charumati, built a temple to Ganesha in Nepal.

Buddhism had its own myth on Ganesha's origin, claiming that Ganesha manifested himself to a mythical king named Vikramji who was blessed by Ganesha in the form of riches.

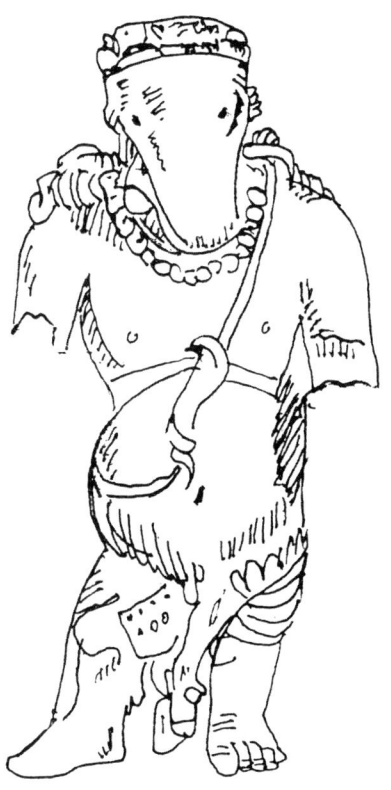

Maha Vinayaka from Gardez Afghanistan

Neither Shiva nor Parvati are credited with his origin either in Buddhism or even in the Nepalese Hindu legends. Although he is not found as a *dwarapala* in North India, he is often presented thus in Nepalese Buddhist monasteries, along with Mahakala. However Ganesha was replaced by Hariti in Chinese Turkestan. The *dwarapala* role is restricted to Nepalese Buddhism.

Ganesha's Nepalese roots have been mentioned earlier. A seated Ganesha with six arms and a fan-shaped *kirita* (probably a stylised five-hooded Naga), holds an unidentifiable object in the upper right hand. This is one of the more *saatvika* images. Another Ganesha stands with a rat under either foot and a five-hooded Naga above him. But the most popular forms in Nepal are Heramba and Shakti Ganesha. The Nepalese Ganesha is best illustrated by a composite deity now in the Museum fur Volkerkunde at Munich. He is ten-armed, holding his and some of Shiva's attributes. He is the five-headed Heramba, above whom the five-hooded Naga has become a stylised fan. His Shakti stands beside him. Beneath his right foot is the lion, and beneath his left, the rat.

One temple north of Thankot contains a Ganesha alongside the Saptamatrika, in Deccani style. Again, reminiscent of the harvest festivals with which he is associated in Central and Western India, there is a custom of a young girl representing Parvati accompanied by two boys, Mahakala and Ganesha, in the Nepalese harvest festivals. We have here a melange of Hindu, Buddhist and Tantric, and northern and southern traditions.

Ganesha is a rare god in Tibet, although a few images have been found. At a few Buddhist monasteries at Tabo, his statue is placed above the entrance. At Lakhang he is painted on the doors.

Ganesha went further north to Khotan (Chinese Turkestan). In a painted panel from Endere, he is four-armed, clad in a tiger skin draped over tight-fitting trousers, dark brown in colour. His head is turned to the right, his trunk to the left. In the figures of this region, Ganesha wears a coronet, but never a *kirita* (crown). Again, the radish is held in one hand.

In the rock-cut temples of Bezaklik, there are several frescoes of Ganesha with six arms, holding the sun, moon, a banner and a *modaka*, with a halo behind his head. At Khaklik, 75 miles from Khotan, there is a painting of an emaciated Ganesha and another of a haloed Ganesha seated on a cushion. Both hold the radish, *modaka* and the goad.

Ganesha reached Mongolia with P'ags-pa, the Tibetan saint mentioned earlier. Here his dancing form, the Nritya Ganapati, was popular, and he is among the 500 gods of Narthan. His left foot is on the rat, the right bent as high as his serpent belt. He wears the five-leafed fan-crown and holds the axe, radish, bowl of sweets and trident (Shiva's symbol) in his four hands.

56   Bronze Ganesha from Nepal

From Chinese Turkestan Ganesha reached China fairly
early. A stone image of A.D. 531 at Kung-hsien is the earliest
Chinese image of Ganesha. He sits cross-legged. Two-
armed, he holds the lotus in the right hand and the
chintamani jewel in the left, as he sits cross-legged in Indian
style. The inscription describes him as the "Spirit King of
the Elephants". Another sixth century representation is a
fresco from the Tun-huang rock-cut caves of Ganesha in the
company of the Sun, Moon and the Navagrahas. Vinayaka,
as he was known in Chinese and Japanese traditions, has
two hands holding the radish and axe. But there was another
form of Ganesha, a double form, known as Kangi-ten.

A secret esoteric form of the god Kangi-ten was derived
from the Tantric cults of Adi Buddha, Maha-Vairochana,
founded on the Yoga doctrine of the union of the Individual
with the Universal Spirit. Kangi-ten was a double Vinayaka,
each embracing the other. The worship of Kangi-ten was
banned by the Chinese emperor Chen Tsung in the
11th century but lived on in Japan.

The worship of Vinayaka was introduced into Japan in the
ninth century by Koloho Daishi. Apart from the radish and
axe, the Japanese Vinayaka also holds the broken tusk.
Another form was Vajra-Vinayaka holding the *vajra* or

57

Stone figure, Sri Lanka

thunder-bolt, while the Kaku-zen-cho form had three heads, each having three eyes, holding a sword, radish, sceptre and *modaka*. The Japanese figures were smiling and even laughing, and were often seated on a mountain. Here Vinayaka was known as the King of Elephants.

Ganesha travelled south to Sri Lanka and east to Burma and South-East Asia. The elephant-headed Gana of the Kantaka Ceting Stupa has been mentioned earlier. Ganesha was and still is a popular figure on the island. A particularly charming image is a four-handed figure carved on a pillar of the Shiva temple at Polonnaruva, holding an axe, noose and a modaka.

Hinduism was a popular religion in Burma in the Gupta period, particularly in lower Burma. Here, Ganesha was the Remover of Obstacles and several small images have been found in this role in Southern Burma. In Northern Burma, several Hindu deities were worshipped in the pagodas, as, for example, the Shwesardaw Pagoda at Pagan where Ganesha is a guardian deity. A remarkable Ganesha was found in the ruins of a Brahmanical temple at Pagan. The god is seated in the *padmaasana*, his four hands holding an axe, rosary and conch, the fourth hand placed on his lap. Ganesha has a crocodile carved on his pedestal, and a tortoise and fish to the right and left of his pedestal in bas-relief. These aquatic associations (including the conch held by him) are quite unique. There are several other Ganeshas in Burma where he was known as Maha-pienne and is still worshipped.

Travelling eastwards, Ganesha went with Burmese Hinduism to Thailand. In the sixth to eighth centuries, Thailand was ruled by the Hindu Mon dynasty who built several temples to Ganesha also. The figures of the early art of Ayuthia are particularly noteworthy for their Indian influence. A beautiful bronze from Ayuthia represents Ganesha seated in the *Maharajalila* pose, the mouse under his uplifted right leg, with a *naga yajnopavita* (snake as sacred thread). Only the noose is recognisable in one hand. As both his tusks are intact, the object in his right hand may be a stylus. This is reinforced by the fact that, in the Hindu temple at Bangkok, Ganesha holds a manuscript in one hand and what has been described as the broken tusk in the other. Obviously the legend of the scribe had travelled thus far.

Cambodia, adjoining Thailand, was totally Indianised and Hindu till the advent, much later, of Buddhism. The country abounds with Hindu gods and temples. An inscription at Angkor Borei, dated A.D. 611 records the grant of slaves to a temple dedicated to several deities, one of whom was Ganesha. A ninth century inscription of Yashovarman I refers to the Ganesha of Chandangiri (Chocung Prey) near which, on a hill, are the ruins of an old Ganesha temple. Another temple of the tenth century is situated at Prasat Bak, besides which several images of the god, known here as Prah Kenes, are scattered all over the country, where he was associated with Shiva, the god of the mountain.

Painted panel from Endere
Chinese Turkestan

The pre-Khmer images are nearly identical to the Gupta Ganesha of Udayagiri, with wide fan-like ears, no neck, no head-dress, no pot-belly, two-armed and with the trunk turned to the left. He wears a *naga yajnopavita*. In the figures of the Khmer period he wears a conical *kirita* (crown). Cambodian Ganeshas are generally two-armed, although four-armed figures have made rare appearances.

Vinayaka from China

Champa, east of Cambodia, was a stronghold of Shaivism. Ganesha travelled with the cult of Shiva to Champa, where early inscriptions refer to Ganesha temples. His popularity was especially marked in the seventh and eighth centuries. An eighth century standing four-armed image of the god (two arms are now missing) recovered at Mi-so'n is one of many Ganesha images, including a seated image in the Saigon museum, of Ganesha, with three deep-set eyes. Buddhist influence may be seen in the protruding *ushnisha* on the head of the god.

Indian contact with Indonesia dates back to the Ramayana which mentions Yava (Java) *dvipa* (island). Shaivism was the predominant religion here. There was no separate cult of Ganesha, but his images have been found in Shiva temples.

The early Ganeshas from Java are extremely primitive and undatable. They represent the elephant-headed one with two arms and no attributes, head-dress or even elephant ears. A very early stone statue from Dieng depicts the deity with four hands holding the axe, rosary, broken tusk and bowl of sweets.

A Javanese variation surrounds Ganesha with skulls, a spin-off of his Shaivite association. A typical representation is a Ganesha from Bara belonging to A.D. 1239, the Singasari period. He is protected from the rear by a face on the back of his head, similar to modern Balinese masks. Skulls are often seen in association with Ganesha in Java. An image from Chandi Singasari replicates this association, for the god sits on a throne in the *maharajalilaasana* pose. A similar standing figure may be seen at Karang Kates. In Java, Ganesha statues may be found at river crossings and other places of danger, probably in his role as the remover of obstacles.

Before the eighth century, all the major Hindu deities were worshipped in Bali. Thereafter, the cult of Shiva gained in popularity. Shiva was generally accompanied by Durga, Ganesha and Nandi. In Bali, Ganesha is generally found standing, with the third eye and the serpent thread.

A statue from Djembaran in South Bali shows Ganesha seated on a throne surrounded by flames, not unlike the Shingon Fudo who took care of royalty after their death and who was depicted as surrounded by flames. This is an unique depiction of Ganesha.

Yet another unique statue was found at Davock Tocket and has been dated to the eighth century. The trunk of this

Ganesha from Polonnaruva, Sri Lanka

59

Ganesha turns directly upwards on level with his *mukuta* (crown). Also, unlike other images from the area who sit with their soles of the feet touching, this figure is in the Indian pose of locked legs, the only one of its kind in this region.

The farthest point to the east travelled by Ganesha was to Borneo, where inscriptions of the fifth century, or earlier, record Hindu rites performed by Brahmins. In a cave at Kombeng containing Brahmanical and Buddhist images in stone, is one of Ganesha, four armed and holding his attributes, of which the axe and rosary are identifiable. The Borneo Ganeshas have nearly straight trunks and a *jataa mukuta* (a hair style in the form of a crown). The Buddhist influence is to be seen in the *urna* or the protuberance between the eyebrows, a mark of greatness. The ears are fan-shaped, the face vertically elongated.

Possibly from Cambodia Ganesha travelled to Mexico and Central America as the elephant-headed god is seen in the form of Virakosa in rare sculptures of that region.

60   *Kangi-ten, double Ganesha, Japan*

Primitive Javanese bronze, British Museum

Java Ganesha, Ethnographic Museum, Leyde

Ganesha from Bali

Pre-Khmer Ganesha, Cambodia

61

62   Stone Ganesha from Bara, East Java

As Hinduism and Buddhism spread through Asia, Ganesha travelled far, appearing in different forms and incarnations. This happened in the Gupta period, making it obvious that his cult had been well established in India long before that period, so that the Indians knew well the god whose cult they were to propagate abroad.

Bronze Ganesha, Borneo

Stone Ganesha from Bara, East Java, rear view

Stone Ganesha, Khmer, Cambodia, Musee Guimet, Paris

63

Dancing Ganesha
Haihaya 11th *c.*
64   Municipal Museum, Allahabad

The worship of divinity in the form of icons or images did not exist in the early period of Hindu civilization. In the early Vedic period, worship consisted of the performance of *yagnas* when offerings were made to the fire. The god of fire, Agni, was believed to carry these oblations to the gods.

However the growth of the concept of Bhakti brought about a transformation, as this involved devotion to a personal deity who became the object of worship. Just as the early Vedic people used Agni or fire to convey their offerings, the devotion to God of *bhaktas* or devotees was now conveyed through the image of a particular deity. Of course *yagnas* are held to this day on important occasions and during the performance of religious functions, but it is the Bhakti form of worship which has dominated religious life during the last 500 years or so.

One of the fundamental beliefs of the Hindu faith is that the soul has no death. It lives on after the death of the body and is reincarnated or reborn by the soul energy entering a new body. In other words, most of us die and are reborn again and again. This cycle of birth, death and rebirth is called *Samsara* and every soul goes through this cycle before attaining *moksha* or liberation. Only the soul which reaches perfection in this life becomes one with the Brahman or the Great Soul and is not reborn on earth.

The aim of life being to break this cycle of birth and death and to attain the Brahman, it was realistically realised by the great Seers of our ancient land that the same path cannot be taken by a philosopher and a man of action, an intellectual and an illiterate, a mystic and a simple man of faith. Therefore three different paths were laid down: Bhakti Yoga (the path of Bhakti or devotion), Karma Yoga (the path of Karma or action) and Gnyana Yoga (the path of wisdom or spiritual enlightenment).

The knowledge of the Vedas and the repeating of Vedic chants while offering oblations to the sacred fire involved an intensive study of the Vedas, which was an intellectual exercise beyond the capability of the majority and was therefore restricted to a few persons in each village or community.

However with the growth of the path of Bhakti and the advent of image-worship, God became easy of access to all.

Also the icon or image served to aid the devotee to concentrate his mind on his beloved deity who was represented by the image. In time, icons were made to represent any form of the Saguna Brahman or Ishwara (God with attributes) in any of His manifestations or *avatars* (incarnations). These images aided devotees to concentrate

Namo Ganapathe thubhyam namo yogaswaroopine

Yogibhyo yogadaathre cha shanthi yogaathmane namah

           (Mudgala Purana)

I bow to that Ganapati who is the very quintessence of yoga

Who teaches yoga to the yogis

And is the living form of Shantiyoga

their minds on God and to enable even the simplest illiterate to practice *dhyana* or meditation, a difficult exercise if God in an abstract form or without form is the object of meditation.

The *pratima* (image or icon) installed for worship in the home or temple is not believed to be God Himself, as often misunderstood by persons of other faiths, but is the *pratika* or symbol of God-head. An apt example often given is of a soldier going to battle carrying his nation's flag which he reveres and protects even with his life. He knows that the flag is not his country but only a symbol representing his country.

In order to denigrate the Hindu religion, the icons or images revered by Hindus were called "idols" by foreign missionaries and treated contemptuously. This has continued to this day with even Hindus calling their images "idols". Hindu icons of worship are as worthy of reverence as the Cross, and images of the Christ and the Madonna and Child seen in a church. The latter would never be permitted to be called idols, and the same objection holds for Hindu icons also.

Images or icons play an important part in the path of Bhakti or devotion. The devotee chooses one or more manifestations of God symbolised in icons or images and keeps them in his home or worships them in a temple.

Images of Ganesha

The Ganesha icon has developed a very rich imagery from the time when it was first fashioned and developed, until today. With the adoption of Ganesha as a powerful deity in the Hindu pantheon, a very rich imagery developed around his icon, despite the fact that the elephant head, ears and trunk are common features not subject to change. Within these limiting factors, it is amazing how different postures, attributes and forms have developed, making Ganesha a most interesting subject of study.

What then are the main characteristics of contemporary Ganesha icons?

Starting with his postures, Ganesha is most often shown in a seated pose, sometimes as a standing figure, and, in the form of Nritya Ganapati, as a dancing figure. If it is in a standing pose, the body is sometimes erect but more often in the *dvibhanga* (two bends) or *tribhanga* (three bends) postures.

In the seated posture, normally the left leg is folded and the right hangs down to the floor level. Sometimes, as in the form of Yoga Ganapati, the legs are crossed in the lotus position with the right foot placed on the left thigh. However the big belly makes such a posture difficult, so that the first position (with one leg dangling) is more common. As for his seat, he is shown seated or standing on a throne-like

Ganesha & Goddess Saraswati
Kota, 18th *c.*, Heras Institute, Bombay

seat, on a carved plank, or on a lotus. He is also shown on his mouse, on a lion or, in a rare case, as the Tantric Moolaadhaara Ganapati, on a multi-headed snake.

Ganesha is shown with two eyes and, in some forms, with three eyes. The trunk is usually turned to the left and in rare figures to the right. In the latter case, he is known as Valamburi Vinayaka in Tamil and is considered very auspicious. With a left-turned trunk he is known as Idamburi Vinayaka. Sometimes he holds a *modaka* (sweet), a *ratna kumbha* (pot of jewels), a pomegranate, a *kamandalu* (prayer vessel), or an *amrita kumbha* (pot of nectar) in his trunk. The trunk is therefore called his fifth hand.

Normally Ganesha is shown with four arms. However he may also be shown with two, six, eight, ten or even sixteen arms, depending on his attributes in the particular role being played.

His unique feature, besides the elephant head, is the large belly practically falling over his lower garment. On his chest, across his left shoulder, is his sacred thread, often in the form of a snake.

Around his abdomen, also as a girdle or belt, is a snake. (See Puranic Legends)

In his hands, Ganesha holds several articles depending on the role he plays and the attributes in each particular incarnation. The main weapons, attributes and articles held in each hand are given in the illustrations on page 83.

As mentioned earlier, Ganapati is considered a Brahmachari (celibate) in most parts of the country. In some areas, Siddhi (achievement) and Buddhi (wisdom) are his symbolic consorts.

However the Tantric religion has a different story to tell as, in Tantricism, sex is an integral part of worship. Ganesha is therefore shown in Tantric icons with one spouse who is his *shakti* or power, whom he fondles. Although Hinduism absorbed the Tantric form of Ganesha, such icons are not normally used for worship but are seen as decorative sculptures on temple walls and pillars.

Ganesha Shrines

Ganesha temples and sculptures can be seen all over the country and in Western and Southern India, practically every village has a shrine and towns and cities abound with them. It is impossible to list them. Also, each one has its own *itihasa*, history and legends, and each temple has an image conforming to the local legend.

It would be interesting to study some of the Ganesha icons popularly worshipped today. For this we may start with Maharashtra, the state where Ganapati worship has led to a rich imagery.

Gajavakthraaya vai thubhyam nairgunyapada dhaarine

Sagunaaya naraakaara kanttaadhasthhaaya thaynamah

(Mudgala Purana)

I bow to you who are the formless Nirguna Brahman (for which you have symbolically donned the elephant's head)

I bow to you who represents- the Saguna Brahman with form (for which below the neck you have donned a human form)

68

Maharashtra's public celebration of the annual festival of Ganesh Chaturthi has few parallels in India (except possibly Durga Pooja in Bengal). But equally important are the innumerable shrines to the elephant-headed god who is greatly loved in this part of the country.

Ashta Vinayak

Of these the most important to Ganesha devotees are the eight Ganesha shrines, the Ashta Vinayak. (Several of the legends pertaining to these shrines are given in Chapter III — Ganesha in Puranic Lore).

These eight forms of Ganesha are *swayambhu,* self-made, and not made by man. This gives added religious significance for Ganesha worshippers. These images are large single pieces of stone (monoliths) in which traces of an elephant-head, trunk and Ganapati's form can be discerned. To the faithful, the powers of these icons is limitless.

These eight shrines are located in Maharashtra. The most popular is the one at Morgaon, south-east of Pune, where Ganesha, riding a peacock and taking the form of **Mayureshwar** or **Moreshwar,** is believed to have destroyed the demon, Sindhu.

Close to Pune, at Theur, is the image of Ganesha as **Chintamani.** Ganesha is believed to have got back the precious *Chintamani* Jewel from the greedy Guna for Sage Kapila at this spot.

At Ranjangaon is the shrine of Ganapati as **Mahaganapati.** The legend here refers to Shiva worshipping Ganesha before fighting the demon, Tripuraasura.

At Siddhatek stands Ganesha as **Siddhivinayak.** It was here that Vishnu was reminded to pray to Ganesha before his fight with the demons, Madhu and Kaitab. By doing so, he achieved success, or Siddhi. This icon has a right-turned trunk.

At Ojhar is the shrine of **Vighnahara** or **Vighneshwara,** a form taken by Ganesha to destroy a demon named Vighnaasura created by Indra.

At Lenyadri nearby is Ganesha in the form of **Girijatmak** or **Girijatmaja,** son of Girija (Parvati). It is believed that Parvati performed penance here to beget Ganapati as her son.

At Pali near the Bombay-Goa road is the shrine of **Ballaleshwar,** where Ganesha saved his devotee, a boy, Ballal, who was beaten up by villagers for his single-minded worship of Vinayaka.

At Mahad, near Khopoli, is the form of Ganesha as **Varad Vinayak,** the giver of bounty and success. A lamp, Nandadeep, is kept permanently lighted here and has been shining since 1892.

Mayureshwar

Chintamani

Mahaganapati

Siddhivinayak

Vighnahara

Girijatmak

Ballaleshwar

Varad Vinayak

71

The Mudgala and Ganesha Puranas, which have glorified Ganapati as the Ultimate Reality, have mentioned many forms of Ganesha images. The former mentions 32 forms befitting the various roles taken by the god.

32 Forms of Ganesha

The main characteristics of the 32 forms are taken from the Dhyana Shlokas and are given below:

1. Bala Ganapati,
   the beloved child

The elephant-faced child is depicted with four arms and is the colour of the rays of the rising sun. He holds a banana, mango, jackfruit and sugarcane in his hands and his favourite sweet, the *modaka,* in his trunk.

2. Taruna Ganapati,
   the youthful Ganesha

The young Ganapati is shown as being red in colour like the noon-day sun. In his hands he holds a noose, an elephant goad, *modaka* sweet, wood-apple, rose-apple, his broken tusk, a sprig of paddy, and a sugar cane branch.

3. Bhakti Ganapati,
   god of devotees

Depicted as being of the colour of the full moon of autumn, in his hands he holds a coconut, mango, banana, and a cup of *payasam* (milk-sweet).

4. Veera Ganapati,
   the valiant warrior

In this form Ganapati is shown with a red complexion, eight pairs of arms and a stern look. In his hands he holds a goblin, spear, bow, arrow, *chakra* (discus), sword, shield, large hammer, *gada* (mace), goad, noose, pick-axe, battle-axe, trident, serpent and banner.

5. Shakti Ganapati,
   the powerful one

Holding in one arm the green-coloured Shakti (power personified in female form), Shakti Ganapati is depicted as being the colour of the sky at sunset. He holds a noose, a garland of flowers and one hand in the *abhaya mudra,* offering blessings to his devotees.

This form of Ganapati is part of Tantric worship.

6. Dwija Ganapati,
   the twice-born

Four-headed, like Brahma, he holds a book, rosary beads, *kamandalu* (vessel used during worship), and a *danda* (staff). He is the colour of the moon and wears lightning-like bangles on his arms.

Shanthiroopaaya shanthaaya shanthidaaya mahodara

Mooshikavaahanaayaiva Gaanapatya priyaaya thay

(Mudgala Purana)

You who are the beloved of the Ganapatyas

You of the large form who has a mouse as his vehicle

You are the embodiment of peace and tranquility, the giver of peace to all!

Bala Ganapati

Taruna Ganapati

Bhakti Ganapati

Veera Ganapati

Shakti Ganapati

Dwija Ganpati

7. **Siddhi Ganapati,**
   god of achievement

Of the colour of golden yellow, he holds a mango fruit, stick of sugarcane, a bunch of flowers and an axe. In his trunk, the fifth hand, he holds a sweetened ball of sesame seeds.

8. **Uchhishta Ganapati,**
   a Tantric deity

Holding Shakti (his female power) in one arm, in his remaining hands he holds a blue lotus, pomegranate, a sprig of paddy, *veena* (musical instrument), and prayer beads. He is depicted as being blue in colour.

9. **Vighna Ganapati,**
   creator of obstacles for the evil

Of golden hue, he is eight-armed and holds, like Vishnu, a *shankha* (conch) and *chakra* (discus). He also holds a sprig of flowers, sugarcane bow, flower arrow, axe, noose and garland.

In this form he is shown adorned with jewelled ornaments.

10. **Kshipra Ganapati,**
    quick-acting god

Handsome of appearance and red in colour like the hibiscus flower, he holds his broken tusk, noose, goad and a sprig of the *kalpavriksha* (wish-fulfilling) tree in his hands and *ratnakumbha* (a pot of precious gems) in his trunk.

11. **Heramba Ganapati,**
    protector of the weak

With five faces and of dark green colour, he rides a lion. Two of his hands are in the *abhaya* (protective) and *varada* (giving) postures. In his other hands he holds a noose, tusk, prayer beads, garland, axe, big hammer, *modaka* sweet and fruit.

12. **Lakshmi Ganapati,**
    giver of success

The goddesses, Siddhi (achievement) and Buddhi (wisdom) in either lap hold blue lotuses in their hands. His one hand is in the *varada* (giving) posture, and in his other hands he has a noose, goad, parrot, a sprig of the *kalpavriksha* tree, *kamandalu* (prayer vessel), sword and pomegranate. In this form he is of pure white colour.

Parashudhaarine thubhyam kamalahasthashobhine

Paashaabhaya dharaayaiva mahodaraaya thay namah

(Mudgala Purana)

You hold an axe in one-hand while a lotus adorns the other

You hold a rope in the third hand and offer protection with the fourth

You of the large form, we bow to you!

Siddhi Ganpati

Uchhishta Ganapati

Vighna Ganapati

Kshipra Ganapati

Heramba Ganapati

Lakshmi Ganapati

13. Maha Ganapati,
    the great one

With a complexion like ripe paddy, he holds his *shakti*, who has a lotus in her hand, on his lap. He has three eyes and the crescent moon on his crown. He holds a pomegranate, *gada* (mace), sugarcane bow, *chakra* (discus), lotus, noose, blue lily, sprig of paddy, tusk, and pot of gems.

This again is a Tantric form.

14. Vijaya Ganapati,
    the giver of success

Of red complexion and riding a rodent, he holds a goad, noose, tusk and mango in his hands.

15. Nritya Ganapati,
    the happy dancer

Of golden colour, Ganapati in this form dances under the *kalpavriksha* tree. He wears rings on his fingers and holds a noose, goad, axe, tusk and sometimes a sweet cake in one of his hands.

16. Urdhva Ganapati,
    Tantric god

Holding a green-complexioned goddess, he holds in his hands a blue flower, sprig of paddy, lotus, sugarcane bow, arrow and tusk. He himself is of golden colour.

17. Ekaakshara Ganapati,
    of the single letter (Gam)

Red in colour, clad in red silk, wearing a garland of red flowers and with the crescent moon on his crown, he is three-eyed with short arms and legs. He carries a pomegranate, noose and goad in his hands. His fourth hand is in the *varada* (wish-giving) pose. He sits in *padmaasana* (yogic lotus pose) and rides the mouse.

18. Vara Ganapati,
    the giver of boons

Of red complexion, he has three eyes and wears the crescent moon on his head. He holds the noose, goad, a dish of honey in his hands, and a pot of jewels in his trunk.

In the Tantric representations of the deity, he is shown with a goddess on his lap.

*Mudaa karaaththa modakam
sadaa vimukthi saadhakam*

*Kalaadharaavathamsakam
vilaasilokarakshakam*

*Anaayakaikanaayakam
vinaashithebhadaityakam*

*Nathaashubhaashunaashakam namaami
tham Vinayakam*

(Adi Shankara)

To him who, with great joy, holds the modaka in his hand

And grants the boon of everlasting salvation

Whose brow is decorated by the crescent moon and who is the protector of the visible world

Who is the leader of the helpless and the destroyer of Gajaasura

Who quickly removes the calamities of his devotees

To that Vinayaka do I bow!

Maha Ganapati

Vijaya Ganapati

Nritya Ganapati

Urdhva Ganapati

Ekaakshara Ganapati

Vara Ganapati

77

19. Tryakshara Ganapati,
    of the three letters AUM (OM)

Of golden colour, he has fly whisks in his flapping ears. He holds a noose, goad, tusk and mango fruit in his hands and a *modaka* sweet in his trunk.

20. Kshipra-Prasada Ganapati,
    who rewards promptly

Adorned with ornaments and seated on a throne of *kusha* grass, in this form his huge abdomen stands out. He holds a noose, goad, lotus, pomegranate, tusk and a sprig of the *kalpavriksha* tree.

21. Haridra Ganapati,
    the golden one

Yellow in colour with bright yellow raiments, he holds a noose, goad, tusk and *modaka* sweet in his hands.

22. Ekadanta Ganapati,
    of the single tusk

Blue in colour and with a huge abdomen, he holds in his hands an axe, rosary beads, *laddu* (a sweet) and his broken tusk.

23. Shrishti Ganapati,
    the creator

Riding a large rodent and of red complexion, he holds in his hands a noose, goad, tusk and mango.

24. Uddanda Ganapati,
    punisher of evil

This Tantric deity carries on his lap his *shakti* (power) a green-coloured female form holding a lotus in her hand. In his ten hands he holds a pot of gems, lotus, blue water lily, *gada* (mace), sugarcane, sprig of paddy, noose, garland, pomegranate and tusk.

Nathetharaathibheekaram
navodithaarkabhaasvaram

Namathsuraarinirjaram
nathaadhikaapaduddharam

Sureshwaram nidheeshwaram
gajeshwaram ganeshwaram

Maheshwaram thamaashraye
paraathparam nirantharam

(Adi Shankara)

He brings fear to those who show no devotion

Yet shines like the rising sun and removes the dangers of his devotees

He is worshipped by both the devas and the asuras

He is the lord of all the gods, master of all kinds of treasures

Head of the elephants and ruler of the ganas

This lord of the Universe, Supreme Being, do I worship always!

78

Tryakshara Ganapati

Kshipra-Prasad Ganapati

Haridra Ganapati

Ekadanta Ganapati

Shrishti Ganapati

Uddanda Ganapati

25. Runamochana Ganapati,
    who releases humanity from bondage

Of white crystal-like mien, he is clad in red silk garments. He holds a goad, noose, rose apple and his tusk in his hands.

26. Dhundhi Ganapati
    of Kashi

Often of *sindura* or red colour, he has prayer beads, his tusk, a *ratnakumbha* (pot of gems) and an axe in his hands.

27. Dwimukha Ganapati,
    the god of two faces

Bluish-green in colour, wearing red silk garments and a gem-studded crown, he holds in his four hands, a noose, goad, tusk and a pot of gems.

28. Trimukha Ganapati,
    the three-faced deity

Seated in the middle of a golden lotus seat with a complexion as red as the *palasa* flower, this form of Ganapati is shown with the left hand in an *abhaya* (protective) pose and the right in the *varada* (reward-giving) pose. He also holds a sharp goad, prayer beads, noose and pot of nectar.

29. Simha Ganapati,
    riding a lion

With the lion as his vehicle, in this form Ganapati is white in colour and also holds a lion in one hand. In his other hands are a sprig of the wish-fulfilling tree, the *veena* (musical instrument), a lotus, a bunch of flowers and a pot of gems.

30. Yoga Ganapati,
    the great yogi

Holding himself in a yogic stance, and bound in a yogic girdle, he is the colour of the early morning sun and wears garments of the blue of Indra. In his hands he holds prayer beads, staff of the yogi, noose and sugarcane.

Samasthalokashankaram
nirasthadaithyakunjaram

Daretharodaram varam
varebhavakthramaksharam

Kripaakaram Kshamaakaram
mudaakaram yashaskaram

Manaskaram namaskrithaam
namaskaromi bhaasvaram

(Adi Shankara)

To him who gives prosperity to all the worlds

And who destroyed the demon Gajamukha

Who is pot-bellied and elephant-faced

Who is merciful and the abode of forgiveness

The abode of joy and the giver of fame and glory

Who leads those who worship him to a virtuous path

80 *To that lustrous one do I bowl*

Runamochana Ganapati

Dhundhi Ganapati

Dwimukha Ganapati

Trimukha Ganapati

Simha Ganapati

Yoga Ganapati

Durga Ganapati

31. Durga Ganapati,
     the saviour

Of a huge body and burnt-gold complexion, he holds prayer beads, an arrow, goad and tusk in his right hands and a noose, bow, flag, and rose apple fruit in his left. His garments are of red colour.

32. Sankatahara Ganapati,
     remover of sorrow

Seated on a red lotus seat and clad in blue, his complexion is that of the rising sun. On his lap he holds his *shakti*, (power) who is of female form, green in colour, holding a blue flower in her hand.

In his hands he holds a goad, noose, and a vessel of *payasam* (milk-sweet). His right hand is in the *varada* or boon-giving pose.

When not in the Tantric form, Sankatahara Ganapati is represented in celibate form.

Sankatahara Ganapati

Attributes of Ganesha

1st row
(1) *paasha* (noose) (2) *ankusha* (elephant goad) (3) broken tusk
(4) goblin (5) Shakti weapon

2nd row
(1) arrow (2) bow (3) *chakra* (discus) (4) knife (5) shield

3rd row
(1) large hammer (2) *gada* (mace) (3) serpent (4) trident (5) pickaxe

4th row
(1) battleaxe (2) banner (3) stick (4) *kamandalu* (vessel used during worship) (5) axe

5th row
(1) bow of sugarcane (2) *shankha* (conch) (3) flower arrow
(4) large axe (5) prayer beads

6th row
(1) fly-whisk fan (2) sword (3) fire (4) *veena* (5) lotus

7th row
(1) bowl of *modaka* (2) sprig of paddy (3) book (4) coconut
(5) flower garland

8th row
(1) sprig of *kalpataru* tree (2) bowl of *payasam* (milk sweet)
(3) *moolaka* (radish) (4) fruits favoured by Ganesha (banana, pineapple, rose apple, wood apple, pomegranate and mango).

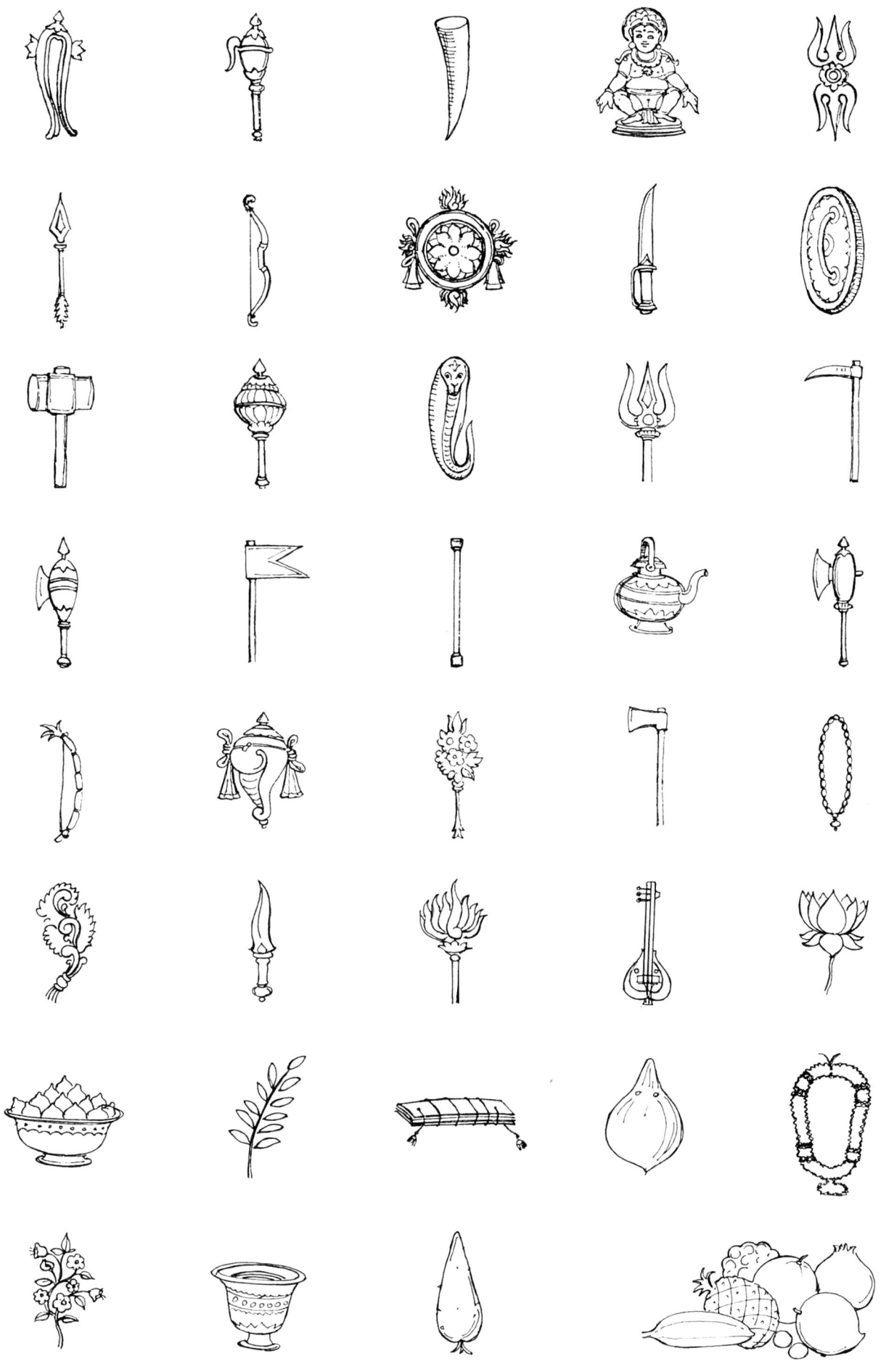

Contemporary forms of Ganesha

Possibly the most modern and contemporary figure amongst Hindu deities is the Ganesha icon. Probably because of his folk origin, there have not been any religious objections when Ganesha icons are given new forms, attributes and new situations. The Ganesha icon is a text book example of the development of Hindu iconography. Just as an ancient people gave him their weapons and objects of veneration, today's devotees give him the weapons of the twentieth century. During the Ganesha festival in Maharashtra, the deity may be seen in modern situations. He is thus the deity who has, most effectively, kept up with the times.

In paintings, oils or water-colour, in metal wall-plaques, in sculpted or carved wood, metal or stone, contemporary artists find great joy in creating modern art and even impressionistic paintings and sculptures of this deity. In living rooms of the well-to-do, on the walls and in prayer-rooms of the middle classes and the poor, one invariably finds some form of Ganapati displayed.

Popular contemporary Ganesha icons or colour prints worshipped in homes are of several forms.

As a Saatvik deity, he holds a lotus and a bowl of modaka (sweets) in two of his hands and his other hands are in the *abhaya* (protective) and *varada* (boon-giving) poses.

The most popular form in which he is represented today is as a benign deity holding an elephant goad, noose and a vessel of *modaka* sweets. The fourth hand is in the protective *abhaya* (do not fear!) pose.

Another popular print has Ganesha in the centre with Goddess Lakshmi, giver of prosperity, on one side and Goddess Saraswati, giver of wisdom, on the other, stressing the close affinity between Ganesha, prosperity and wisdom.

In the south, a popular framed print seen in pooja rooms has the Shiva family gathered together as in a family photograph. Shiva and Parvati are seen seated on a throne with their sons, Ganesha and Kumara, on either side. At their feet are Nandi, Shiva's bull, the mouse, Ganapati's vehicle, and the peacock, the vehicle of the second son, Kumara (popularly called Murugan by the Tamils).

*Akimchanaarthimaarjanam
chiranthanokthibhaajanam*

*Puraaripoorvanandanam
suraarigarvacharvanam*

*Prapanchanaashabheeshanam
dhananjayaadibhooshanam*

*Kapoladaanavaaranam
bhaje puraanavaaranam*

(Adi Shankara)

To the one who removes the sorrows of the downtrodden

And is the subject of those who sing the ancient Vedas

Who is the elder son of Shiva and destroyer of the Asura's pride

Who frightens those who destroy the world

And is the jewel of heroes like Arjuna by whom he is adored

From whose face flows nectar

To this ancient timeless Gajaanana do I bow!

1. Vinayaka
   Ivory figure — late 19th *c.*

2. Marble Ganesha
   Porbandar, Gujarat

3. Trimukha Ganapati
   Wooden carving

3

1

2

Bronze Ganesha in Shiva Tandava pose

Ceramic Ganapati
Modern art

Veena Ganapati
Symbol of Nada Brahma

Brass Ganesha
Light-hearted contemporary figure

The making of the Ganesha icon

The materials out of which Ganesha icons are made are of an unbelievably wide range.

Temple images are often monolithic, carved out of a single stone. In the north, marble figures are popular, in the west the images are usually painted red (the colour of saffron) and in the south, they are mostly of black stone, oiled and made shiny.

For home worship during Ganesh Chaturthi in the south, often an unbaked mud figure is purchased, and, after *pooja*, immersed in the sea, river, tank or well where it melts to form part of the waters. Nowadays, however, clay figures of Ganapati, baked and painted in multi-colours, are used for the same purpose.

In Maharashtra, and in recent years, in other parts of the country, mammoth figures of the god are worshipped in public places and taken out in procession during Ganesh Chaturthi, each street vying with the other in the size of the image. In addition, new legends with a contemporary ambience are invented which add to the excitement. During wars, for example, Ganesha is shown encouraging Indian *jawans*. Scenes from the Indian independence movement with important political leaders often form part of the scene. Each year brings forth new themes for tableaux built around the massive form of Ganapati. Common themes however are the reenactment of stories from the Puranas.

Artistic representations of Ganesha are very popular today. Elaborate carvings of different types of wood are sometimes polished and painted, but most often left in the natural form.

In Ganesha images of ivory and sandalwood, usually made of single pieces of the material, exquisitely minute details are carved which are evidence of the skill of the workmen.

Some of the most beautiful icons are those made of brass, bronze and copper. Silver images, either solid or silver-plated, are used by the well-to-do for worship in homes.

Semi-precious stones like coral, jade, sphatika (crystal), quartz, etc. are carved as Ganesha figures. Also gem-encrusted gold jewellery forms of Ganesha have a long history of the jewellers' excellence in artistic creations.

Granite, soap-stone, ceramics, papier mache and plaster of Paris (and, today plastic also) are some of the other materials used for fashioning icons. Mud, sand from an ant-hill, stone from banks of sacred rivers, *durva* and *kusha* grass, the fig tree and sandal paste are some of the materials also used to make images for special occasions.

Ganesha
Kalamkari print, A.P.

Equally interesting are other folk art representations, a rare one made of the bark of a tree and others of mud or burnt brick carved and baked in a brick kiln.

Paintings on cloth and canvas and miniature paintings are popular in Rajasthan and go back to the 16th century in design, though many are painted today. Kalamkari folk paintings of Andhra Pradesh cover a wide range of Ganesha forms.

Tanjore paintings, gold and semi-precious stone-encrusted, and Mysore paintings decorated with gold foil are some of the most artistic of today's creations.

Paintings of Ganesha by both well-known and little-known artists are printed on a mass-scale (often in garish colours)

Nritya Ganapati
Somnathpur, 13th *c.*

and sold near temples, at shopping centres and roadside
shops, as are calendar reprints.

Villagers embroider folk art figures of Ganesha on cloth.
Equally skilled are paintings on silk or tussore.

Ganesha figures and plaques made of wood and inlaid with
ivory and woods of many colours are very popular, as are
metal plaques beaten into Ganesha forms.

In fact it can be stated without hesitation that whichever
material is used, whether the images are carved, painted,
etched or embroidered, the artistic and religious zeal of
the artist stands out as a contemporary homage to this
great god.

90 *Soapstone Ganesha*

The Vedas and the Upanishads teach the highest truths known to mankind. They contain the essence of the philosophical background of Hinduism, and the profound truths taught in them guide Man in his search for spiritual enlightenment. Study of these scriptures involves a high degree of erudition and knowledge, followed by meditation on each word and each thought. Naturally only a small number of people have the intellectual background and the time and inclination to spend on such in-depth and intensive study.

To the majority, even understanding these scriptures becomes an impossible task and therefore symbolic methods of education have been devised by our ancients. Symbols are really a means of communication in a simplified form.

Through stories from the epics, the Ramayana and the Mahabharata, and from the Puranas, for example, word-pictures of events were drawn which symbolise the truths of the Upanishads. By means of these symbolic stories, what is good and evil, right and wrong are taught in a down-to-earth form. These stories have been imparted to successive generations by word of mouth, as bed-time stories told to grandchildren by grandmothers, in the form of *kirtans* or songs sung by wandering minstrels, as dances performed in temples, and by carvings of Puranic stories on temple walls. Through music and dance, the arts of story-telling, painting and sculpture, the mysteries of life in this world and thereafter were symbolically conveyed in a simplified form. Knowledge of the Brahman, the One God, a study of Dharma, the righteous duties to be followed by men and women, the practice of Nishkaama Karma or selfless action, and what is necessary to set up a value-based society have all been conveyed through these symbolic stories. Thereby the uneducated and illiterate are able to understand philosophical concepts as easily as the knowledgeable ones.

Every manifestation of God and Nature has been turned into a symbol. A large tree, for example, becomes a symbol to show God's protection by the shade it gives to the high and low, without differentiation. Stories of *vanadevata* (forest gods) dwelling in the trees prevent their wanton destruction. The wheel, the mud pot, the conch, the lotus, the fruit, the seed, each has become an aesthetic symbol of a spiritual truth. Similarly every other creation of God on earth.

Taking the next step into symbolism, as mentioned earlier, the abstraction of the Manifest Spirit, Nirguna Brahman, without shape, form or attributes, was difficult of comprehension by the majority. The Saguna Brahman was symbolised by each of the Trinity, their consorts or families and the various *avatars* (incarnations) holding different articles in their hands and presented in various postures symbolising the act they are performing in that particular

Nithaanthakaanthadanthakaanthim anthakaanthamaathmajam

Achinthyaroopam anthaheenam antharaayakrinthanam

Hridanthare nirantharam vasanthameva yoginaam

Thamekadantameva tham vichinthayaami santhatham

(Adi Shankara)

To him who is adorned with shining ivory teeth

And is the son of Shiva the destroyer of Yama

Whose infinite form is beyond Man's comprehension

Who is the destroyer of obstacles and is ever present in the hearts of Yogis

On him with the single tusk do I contemplate and meditate always!

role. For example, Ganapati in the form of Heramba Ganapati protects his devotees. In the form of Veera Ganapati he is the warrior who destroys evil and as Sankatahara Ganapati, he removes sorrow. For each role, he holds different articles in each hand. These are his attributes, symbolic of the powers that he uses in that particular role.

Symbolism of the Ganesha form

The Puranic legends explaining the form of Ganesha, his birth, elephant head, broken tusk and mouse-vehicle have been narrated earlier. Also his origin and the development of his icon in art, history and archaeology through the ages in India and abroad.

The most interesting facet of the Ganesha icon however is the symbolism attached to it, as these symbols serve the purpose of communicating the purpose of the avatar of Ganapati, to convey the philosophical truths behind the faith in this deity in an understandable form, and to translate the values of the culture symbolically.

Ganesha, the son of Shiva and Parvati, is the first deity to be worshipped, as he is the remover of obstacles.

The most striking feature is his huge body which is symbolic of the Cosmos or the Universe. The gods and all mankind, all living things and all manifestations of Nature are encompassed within it. The large size is indicative of the role

he plays as one within whom the whole universe is contained. Ganesha in the form of Vishwaroopa where his body covers the whole universe shows the importance of this deity who is the Universe itself.

The most striking feature of Ganesha is his elephant head. According to the Puranas, the head of a boy was removed and replaced by an elephant's head, symbolic of auspiciousness, strength and intellectual prowess. All the qualities of the elephant are contained in the form of Ganapati. The elephant is the largest and strongest of animals of the forest. Yet he is gentle and, amazingly, a vegetarian, so that he does not kill to eat. He is very affectionate and loyal to his keeper and is greatly swayed if love and kindness are extended to him. Ganesha, though a powerful deity, is similarly loving and forgiving and moved by the affection of his devotees.

The elephant can destroy a whole forest and is a one-man army when provoked. Ganesha is similarly most powerful and can be ruthless when containing evil.

Again, Ganesha's large head is symbolic of the wisdom of the elephant. His large ears, like the winnow, sift the bad from the good and the essential truths are conveyed to his worshippers. His large ears also point out that Vedic thought and ideas can be learnt only when listened to at the feet of a *guru*. They then have to be pondered upon for which wisdom, symbolised by his large head, is necessary.

The most interesting feature of Ganesha is his trunk which represents OM or the Pranava Mantra, the sound from which the world was created. Ganesha himself is believed to be the embodiment of OM and the curved trunk (*vakratunda*) is symbolic of the Pranava. In fact the Devanagari symbol of OM (ॐ) is believed to resemble the elephant and his extended trunk. Similarly the Tamil OM (ௐ) has the appearance of an elephant's head and hanging trunk.

Ganesha's trunk is symbolic of his *viveka* or discrimination, a most important quality necessary for the spiritual progress of a Vedantin. The elephant uses its trunk to push down a massive tree, carry huge logs to the river and for other heavy tasks. The same huge trunk is used to pick up a few blades of grass, to break a small coconut, remove the hard nut and eat the soft kernel inside. The biggest and minutest of tasks come within the range of this trunk which is symbolic of Ganesha's intellect and its powers of discrimination.

The broken tusk which goes against all canons of orderliness, balance and symmetry, which are part of Hindu thought, is an unusual facet of Ganesha. Symbolically Ganesha breaking his tusk to fight with a demon or to write the Mahabharata signifies the great sacrifice which Divine Beings make for aiding mankind. It also shows that Ganesha is beyond the rules of Cosmic orderliness as he is the Cosmos itself.

The huge paunch and his voracious appetite are seen in the story of Kubera's feast (See Puranic Lore). It symbolically shows that God is never appeased or pleased by wealth. It is finally a few grains of rice given with love that quelled his craving to eat.

The huge belly also signifies that Ganesha swallows the sorrows of the Universe and protects the world.

The awkward and corpulent body of Ganesha is symbolic of God's lesson to us that beauty of the outward form has no connection with inner beauty and spiritual perfection.

The mouse, Ganesha's vehicle, is a rodent of great nuisance value to the farmer. It is shown at the feet of his master constantly nibbling away. The mouse symbolises the petty desires of men which nibble away at their personalities and their inner selves.

All deities are symbolically given several arms and hands. Only the natural arms (the two in front) have hands found in "action" poses, such as the *abhaya* (protective) *mudra*, and *varada* (boon-giving) *mudra*. The other hands symbolise the different attributes of the deity, and the various roles taken by him.

Ganesha is normally shown with one hand in the *abhaya* pose and the second holding a *modaka* sweet symbolic of the sweetness of the realised Inner Self. In the two hands behind him he often holds an *ankusha* (elephant goad) and a *paasha* (noose). The noose is to convey that worldly attachments and desires are a noose. The goad is to prod Man to the path of righteousness and truth. He sometimes holds the broken tusk in one hand, symbolic of knowledge and erudition, as he used it to write the Mahabharata. Equally important to Ganesha is the sugarcane, the elephant's favourite food and like the Eternal Truth, it is outwardly hard of attainment, but once reached, the inner layers are infinitely sweet, as sweet as the sugar in the cane.

Ganesha is shown with other attributes depending on the roles taken by him in his various *avatars*. For destroying demons of evil, he may hold two or more of several weapons. Some of the common ones are a trident, spear, knife, bow, arrow, discus, sword, shield, hammer, mace, snake, Shakti weapon (double trident), large axe, pickaxe, battleaxe, baton, conch, dagger, and stick of fire.

Other attributes seen in his hands in more peaceful roles are a banner, prayer vessel, pot of nectar, pot of gems, prayer beads, flower garland, fly-whisk, *veena*, fruits of various kinds, a sprig of grain, a bunch of flowers, the lotus, radish, book, a branch of the wish-fulfilling *kalpavriksha* tree and others. (The *veena* is symbolic of Nada-Brahmam, the music and rhythm of the Cosmos. The lotus is a symbol of purity as it grows in muddy waters but is untouched by the dirt from which it emerges).

Ganapati Festival, Bombay
Painted clay image

Rajasthani folk art

Pattachitra painting, Orissa

The Shiva family
Calendar print

95

Yoga Ganapati

The Dance of Creation
Ganesha under the Kalpavriksha tree

Vinayaka with Goddesses Lakshmi and Saraswati
Calendar print

Ganesha is sometimes shown with three eyes. The two front eyes symbolise the power of Surya (the sun) and Chandra (the moon). The third eye is believed to be symbolic of Agni, the powerful god of fire. It is located at the seat of wisdom, the centre of the forehead.

Ganesha sometimes wears the 3rd day crescent moon on his head. Symbolically this crescent without blemishes leads human beings to attain pure knowledge and spiritual enlightenment.

The snake worn around Ganesha's stomach is symbolic of cosmic energy. It is sometimes worn by him as a sacred thread across his left shoulder.

As can be seen, nearly every aspect and role of Ganesha has meanings and interpretations by which the wisdom of this great god is conveyed to his devotees in the easiest way possible by means of symbols and their messages.

98   Seated Ganesha, Mysore painting

The worship of Divinity through images and icons is part of Bhakti Yoga.

Bhakti itself has two aspects — Para and Apara Bhakti. In Para Bhakti, the higher stage, the devotee is consumed with love for his Ishta-Devata, his personal deity. He is intoxicated by this love. He performs no rituals but through Ekaanta Bhakti, or single-minded devotion, he sees his Ishta-Devata everywhere. Saints and mystics are part of this form of Bhakti and ultimately become one with Divinity.

The other aspect followed by the majority is Apara Bhakti where the devotee chooses a personal deity, called the Ishta-Devata, to whom he offers worship and in whose name he performs rituals.

Ganesha worshippers of the latter category are found all over India, predominantly in Maharashtra and Tamil Nadu.

To start with, the devotee selects an icon or painting of this deity and places it in his home in a mini-temple-like structure facing the rising sun.

In front of the image, *rangoli (kolam)* designs are decoratively drawn on the floor.

Often a *swastika* is drawn as part of the design, as this auspicious sign is associated with Ganesha, god of auspiciousness. Lamps are then lighted in front of the image which symbolise the illumination of the mind with knowledge.

In its simple form, the worshipper sits in meditation in front of the icon, concentrating his mind on it in Dhyana Yoga. Some perform *japa* (which means reciting aloud or in one's mind repeatedly one or more *mantras* or prayer hymns). Great concentration of the mind is needed to keep one's mind on the deity, but such worship is probably the best as it is simple and leads to spiritual wakening.

The simple mantras which help in meditation are the Ekaakshara Mantra (Om Gam Ganapataye Namah), based on the single syllable Gam, the *beejaakshara* or seed syllable of the word, Ganapati, the Ashtaakshara Mantra (Om Shri Ganeshaaya Namah) and other Ganapati Mantras.

These mantras are considered to be so powerful that even the gods chant them. Sage Vyasa is believed to have written the Puranas only after meditating on the Ekaakshara Mantra.

For those who prefer ritualistic worship there are various paths. Pilgrimages to Ganesha shrines, visits to temples, taking part in feasts and festivals are part of this form of Bhakti.

Mahaaganesha pancharatnam aadarena yonvaham

Prajalpathi prabhaathake hridi smaran Ganeshwaram

Arogathaam adoshathaam susaahitheem suputhrathaam

Samaahithaayurashtabhoothim-abhyupaithi sochiraath

(Adi Shankara)

Whoever recites daily the Pancharatna stotra early in the morning

Meditating on Ganesha with respect and regard

Will be free of disease and blame

He will enjoy wealth and prosperity The gift of noble children

And the great gift of poetry and knowledge till the end of his life.

Performing rituals at home or in temples is the other path chosen by the faithful.

The ritual could be very simple, with the devotee performing *pooja* or worship by offering a few flowers and leaves and burning camphor before the icon.

Before the commencement of all *poojas* in the south, the worshipper knocks the two ends of his forehead (believed to be the spots connecting nerves to the intellect), with clenched fists, saying the mantra, "Shuklaambharadharam . . . " (see page 1), thereby invoking Ganapati, the god of the intellect.

At roadside shrines in the south, a common sight is of worshippers knocking on the ends of the forehead followed by *thoppukaranam,* (a form of *baithak* with arms crossed across the chest, the hands holding the ear tips, while the devotee squats and rises several times). This is a form of self-imposed penance, praying for forgiveness.

For those desiring elaborate rituals as part of their offering, what is known as the Shodacha-Upachaara Pooja (worship by 16 offerings) is performed.

Tantric Moolaadhaara Ganapati
on a 5-headed snake

The 16 steps involve first, the invocation of the deity, then the sprinkling of water and sipping it. The icon is given fresh garments and a sacred thread. Sandalwood paste, fragrant *agarbatti* (incense sticks) and garlands are used to adorn the image. Flowers are offered accompanied by *mantras.* Then *archana* is performed by repeating either 21, 108 or 1000 names of Ganesha, offering a flower or leaf with each name. Food cooked in the home is offered as also fruits, coconut, betel leaves and betelnuts *(supari).*

Incense, lights and camphor are burnt and waved before the deity followed by *pradakshina* (circumambulation) and the offering of flowers.

Each of these acts is symbolic. Sprinkling of water and sipping it suggests purification of oneself and the surroundings. The offering of flowers is done by picking them up with all five fingers (symbolic of our five senses). They are brought near the heart and then placed at the foot of the icon. This symbolises the offering of one's *atma* (soul), mind and heart to God. Food from the house is offered as thanksgiving for God's bounty. The breaking of the coconut symbolises the destruction of one's ego. The offering of coconut and betel leaves (symbolising fertility) is to ask God for the blessing of children for the home.

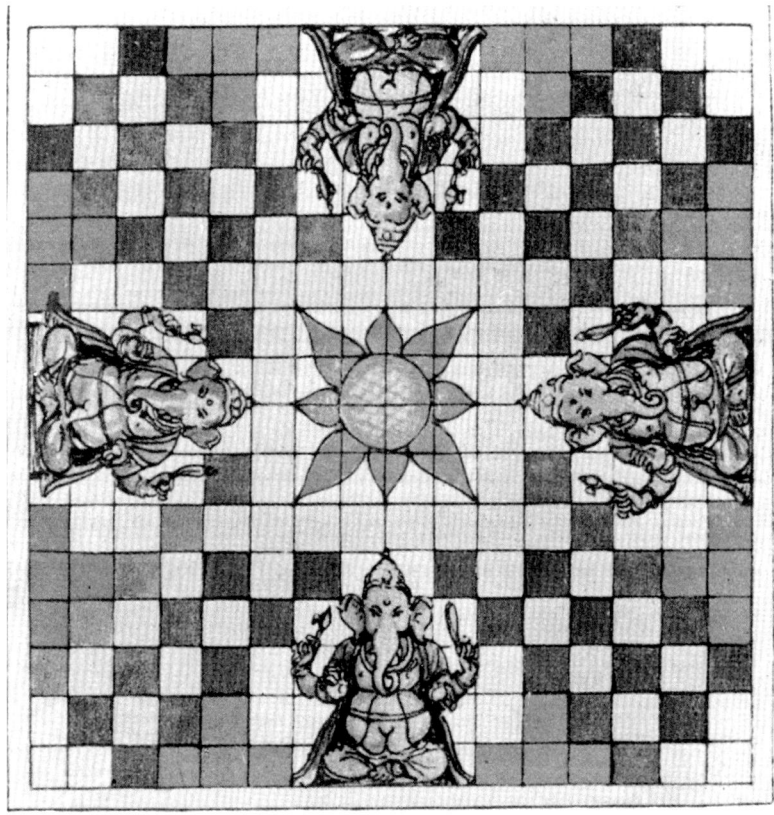

Incense symbolises the fragrance of God's love and the burning of camphor is for the destruction of our egos and arrogance. The waving of camphor before the deity, called *aarti*, symbolises the surrender of the worshipper to the will of God. Bells are rung to keep out other noises during *aarti* and as a means of celebration. The worshipper walks around the icon thrice clock-wise (following the earth's movement round the sun) to symbolically cross the nether regions, the earth and the heavens to reach God.

The form of Ganesha used for prayer need not be an image or icon. Any symbol suffices. A small pyramid of turmeric (mixed with water) is often kept on a betel leaf and worshipped. Even sand or mud blobs will do. Often a pot *(kumbha)*, on which thin string is criss-crossed, symbolises Ganapati. It is filled with water (symbolically supposed to be from the 7 sacred rivers). Five mango leaves (the five senses) and a coconut, beloved of Ganesha, are placed at the mouth of the pot. The pot is then placed on a platform of rice and used for prayer.

Panchabhoota Ganapati

Except the *ketaki* flower *(thaazhambu)* and *tulsi* leaves, all flowers and leaves are offered to Ganesha. The lotus, *champa*, jasmine, rose, *kusha* and *durva* grass, herbal leaves, *bilva* leaves are all equally loved by him. Usually 21 varieties of flowers and leaves are used when performing elaborate *poojas.* For the *naivedyam* (food offering), all types of sweets, especially the *modaka,* coconut, jaggery, all varieties of fruits (especially those liked by elephants), rice and lentils are offered.

Tuesdays and Fridays are special days for Ganesha *vratas* (penances).

Based on a legend, young girls, especially in Tamil Nadu perform Tuesday *vrata* for a whole year as it is believed that this brings them good husbands and happy homes.

On Fridays women perform Ganesha worship before sunrise after which they repeat a story about Ganesha to other women. This is believed to bring special spiritual benefits.

Another day sacred for rituals is Sankatahara Chaturthi, for the removal of all sorrows.

Ganapati is also worshipped in a special pooja for a *mandala* (40 to 45 days, usually 41 days). After initiation by a *guru,* a square surface is prepared on a platform or on *durva* grass and 196 small squares of different colours are etched on it with rangoli powder, as also four colourful Ganapati figures on four sides and a lotus in the centre. On the lotus is placed a *kumbha* (pot of water), after which *mantras* are chanted.

Tantrics perform this ritual by substituting the pot by a Tantric *yantra*, a copper plate with mystic diagrams etched on it, and then recite tantric *mantras*.

Ganesha vachanam shruthva pranathaa bhakthi bhaavathah

Paprachchustham punah shaanthaa gnyaanam broohi Gajaanana

(Ganesha Geetasara)

Listening to the words of Ganesha
With prayer and devotion, we ask again—
Teach us the knowledge of peace, oh Gajanana!

103

Tantrics also worship Ganesha as Moolaadhaara Ganapati, standing on a 5-headed snake or sitting on the *moolaadhaara chakra* and holding a bell in his trunk. The arousal of *kundalini* power is associated with this form of Ganesha.

Another form worshipped by Tantrics is of Ganesha as Panchabhoota Ganapati, dividing his body into the five elements, shown by a rectangle, circle, triangle, crescent and flame, representing the earth, water, fire, air and ether.

The great day for Ganesha however is Ganesh Chaturthi on the fourth day of the bright fortnight in Bhaadrapad (or the month of Aavani of the Tamils). The celebrations on this day have reached gargantuan proportions in Bombay and similar celebrations are now being held in towns and cities in other parts of India. Huge images of Ganesha are specially made for this festival and worshipped. After several days, they are taken in procession amidst music and dancing, and then left in the sea or river, to become one with the elements.

God of Auspiciousness . . . the Beginning of all Beginnings

Ganesha is, in one way, the most complex of concepts. Except as an incarnation on earth, neither God nor His forms as the Trinity or their consorts are ever "born". God only exists. Ganesha, alone of the deities, was mind-born or created and acquired as a son by Shiva and Parvati.

Yet, amazingly, he is also the simplest, as he is the god of all people, big and small, educated and illiterate. For him, no formalised form of worship is necessary. Meditating on him results in filling one's heart with love of one's fellow-beings, human and animal, which is after all the aim of true religion.

This god of wisdom teaches that the path to success and achievement is through the use of the intellect, and that through wisdom alone can one reach salvation. (This great truth is called the Vinayaka Tattvam).

The calm and majestic Ganesha with the strength and power of an elephant is the Lord of all obstacles which keep Man under control, and yet is also the remover of the obstacles which befuddle Man in his endeavours. Like the elephant he has a prodigious memory, and never forgets the qualities of loyalty and devotion of those around him.

He spreads the message of peace and tranquility and his large size therefore evokes great love, never fear. In fact his unusual form gets embedded in the mind of the worshipper.

Vinayaka Deepam

Ganesha is the embodiment of OM, the symbol of the Great
God, and is the delight of the gods and the beloved of
humanity. He is the playful god of the young and the great
guru of the old. He is the god of auspiciousness, the
beginning of all beginnings, the saviour of all that is good.

With the rishis of yore his devotees therefore join and sing —

Sadaa Brahma bhootam vikaaraadi heenam
Vikaaraadi bhootam Maheshaadivandyam
Apaaraswaroopam svasamvedyamekam
Namaamah sadaa Vakratundam bhajaamah

(He who is a form of the Eternal Spirit, the Brahman
Is changeless yet causes change all round
Him whom Mahesha and the other gods worship
Who has a unique form and deep knowledge of the Self
This Vakratunda do we worship always).

OM Shantih, Shantih, Shantihi!
(OM Peace, Peace, Peace unto all!)

Bibliography

Title	Author	Publisher
5000 years of the Art of India	M. Bussagli & C. Sivaramamurthi	Harry N. Abrams Inc., New York
Ganapati (Tamil publication)		Thiruvaduthurai Aadheenam, Thiruvaduthurai
Ganesha	Alice Getty	Munshiram Manoharlal, New Delhi
Glory of Ganesha		Central Chinmaya Mission Trust, Bombay
Hindu Mythology	WJ. Wilkins	Rupa & Co., New Delhi
Hinduism — An Introduction	Shakunthala Jagannathan	Vakils, Feffer & Simons Ltd., Bombay
Iconography of the Hindus, Buddhists and Jains	R.S. Gupte	D.B. Taraporevala Sons & Co. Pvt. Ltd., Bombay
Imprints of Indian Thought and Culture Abroad		Vivekananda Kendra Prakashan, Madras
India's Contribution to World Thought & Culture	Edited by Lokesh Chandra	Vivekananda Rock Memorial Committee, Madras
Mudgala Purana Stotras		T.S. Rajagopalan, Madras
Stotramala (Tamil)	Edited by Dr. S.S. Raghavan	Giri Trading Agency, Madras
The Art of India	C. Sivaramamurthi	Harry N. Abrams Inc., New York
The Cultural Heritage of India		R.K. Mission Institute of Culture, Calcutta
The Development of Hindu Iconography	J.N. Banerjee	Munshiram Manoharlal, New Delhi
The Elements of Hindu Iconography	T.A. Gopinatha Rao	Indological Book House, Varanasi
The Popular View of Ganesha in Madras	K. Srikanta Iyer	Indian Antiquary XXX
The Problem of Ganapati	Rev. H. Heras	Indological Book House, Delhi
Vaishnavism, Saivism and Minor Religious Sects	R.G. Bhandarkar	Asian Educational Services, New Delhi

Other Books in the Introduction Series

HINDUISM — An Introduction
Shakunthala Jagannathan

BALAJI VENKATESHWARA — An Introduction
Shakunthala Jagannathan

SHIVA — An Introduction
Devdutt Pattanaik

VISHNU — An Introduction
Devdutt Pattanaik

LAKSHMI — An Introduction
Devdutt Pattanaik

DEVI — An Introduction
Devdutt Pattanaik

HANUMAN — An Introduction
Devdutt Pattanaik

NANAK — An Introduction
Purushottam Nijhaawan